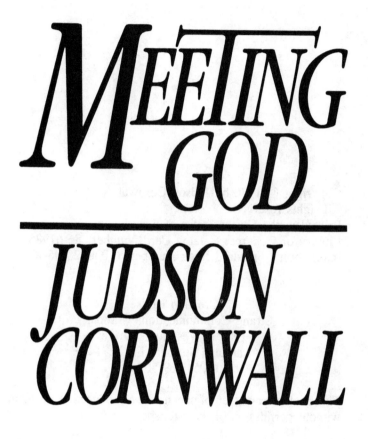

MEETING GOD

JUDSON CORNWALL

Creation House
Strang Communications Company
Altamonte Springs, Florida

Creation House
Strang Communications Company
190 N. Westmonte Drive
Altamonte Springs, FL 32714
(305) 869-5005

Unless otherwise identified, Scripture quotations are from the New King James Version of the Bible, copyright 1982 by Thomas Nelson Inc., Nashville, Tennessee. Used by permission.

Quoted material from *Those Who Love Him* by M. Basilea Schlink (English edition published by Zondervan Corporation) used by permission of author.

ACKNOWLEDGEMENT

My deepest appreciation to my wife, Eleanor, without whose gentle encouragement and support I would have found the writing of this book a laborious chore.

My earnest thanks to my secretary, Cheryl Tipon, who did much of the research for this book, the initial editing and the typing of the manuscript. Her critique and input contributed much to the development of the book.

Our united labors present this book to you, the reader.

DEDICATION

To Cheryl Tipon, a follower of Christ,
a filial friend, a fellow-laborer in my ministry,
a faithful secretary and a forbearing
editor of my writings.

CONTENTS

Acknowledgement 5
Dedication 7
Preface 11
Chapter 1   Adam Completely Knew God 15
Chapter 2   Noah Met a Speaking God 29
Chapter 3   Abraham Met a
             Covenant-Keeping God 51
Chapter 4   Moses Met a Moral God 73
Chapter 5   Joshua Met an Almighty God 95
Chapter 6   Isaiah Met a Holy God 115
Chapter 7   Ezekiel Met the Glory of God 133
Chapter 8   Daniel Met a Revealing God 157
Chapter 9   Peter Met the God-Man 181
Chapter 10   John Met a Loving God 205
Chapter 11   Paul Met the Indwelling God 223

PREFACE

I frequently say that worship extols God for who He is, in contrast to praise, which eulogizes God for what He has done. If this definition is correct, then worship is always limited to our knowledge of God, for we cannot extol God beyond our concepts of Him. This would explain some of the very shallow expressions of worship that are so common in our churches. I cannot help feeling that many American Christians are more interested in the principles of God than in the person of God. They give to God, receive from God and work on His behalf, but they never enter into an intimate relationship with Him. This is far beneath God's desires and design for redeemed persons, for the cry of the twenty-four elders in heaven is "You were slain, and have redeemed us to God by Your blood" (Rev. 5:9).

God planned the complete restoration of persons for both His own sake and for the sake of humanity. God purposed to bring mankind back into personal relationship with Himself, but the route was a long one, for the distance between men and God was great, and the necessary knowledge of God was lost to men. Far more than mere forgiveness was needed—for that could have been totally an act of God—but mankind needed a change of mind about God, and that required man's cooperation. Little wonder, then, that it has taken so long: whenever God chooses to submit His purposes to our participation, a conflict of wills flares up in a conflict that causes the entire program either to grind to a screeching halt or, at best, slow to a snail's pace.

That God created Adam and Eve as love objects with whom He could have fellowship is the philosophy of all Scripture, and His ultimate success is pictured in the first two chapters of Genesis. Through daily fellowship with God, Adam came into an awareness of God and a knowledge of His nature unsurpassed throughout the history of mankind, but sin erased this knowledge as surely as pressing the "delete" key on a computer completely removes the information that was on the screen. Adam had not learned about God through his natural intellect. Spiritual things are spiritually discerned; this first man learned of God by a communication from God's Spirit to his spirit, not by what his senses perceived or his mind rationalized.

But sin caused Adam and Eve's expulsion from the garden, and the loss of contact with God appears to have cost them their knowledge of God. They forfeited access to the tree of life, and the workings of death began in their minds. They didn't even retain sufficient knowledge of God in their memory circuits to instruct their children properly. Sin, which is rebellion against

God, leaves a person devoid of any knowledge of God, but leaves a deep longing in the soul. We all have a void that craves satisfaction, but how to fulfill that craving is beyond our knowledge. Most people invest their entire lifetimes in this pursuit, but only those who meet Jesus—God's provision of restoration—ever find the satisfaction they have craved.

What Adam lost in a moment has taken centuries to restore to humanity. Little by little, and in person after person, God has placed back in the spirit of men the knowledge of Himself that makes worship and fellowship possible and pleasurable. Through Noah, God restored the knowledge that He enjoys communication with people. Abraham entered into that communication and learned that God is also a God of covenants. Years later, Moses, having participated in these two revelations of God, discovered that God is a moral God concerned with man's good, and Joshua experienced the almightiness of God. This formed a basis for further revelations, so that Isaiah met a holy God, Ezekiel met a glorious God, and Daniel met a revealing God.

With this much revelation of Himself available to mankind, God chose to come among us once again; Peter met the God-man in Jesus, while John met the love of God in Christ. After Paul's conversion on the Damascus road, he was granted the revelation that the God who had daily come to be with Adam has now come to be in His chosen people. We need not wait until "the sweet by and by," "when we all get to heaven," to know the God who was so real and personal to Adam; ever since Adam walked in the garden, God has been giving back to men that wonderful knowledge of Himself, until we now have the second Adam in us as the hope of glory. God may not walk with us in the flesh, but He is even closer to us as He indwells our spirits.

What a great debt of gratitude we Christians owe to these pilgrims who blazed a trail into the knowledge of God that allows us to worship Him both in spirit and in truth. They did not discover God; God revealed Himself to them, but they moved into their revelations and lived them out in everyday life, and they communicated their revelations so that succeeding generations could enter into them. Each revelation was one rung higher on the ladder that reaches from earth to heaven. Christians determine by their actions just how close to God they choose to be. At whatever point they stop climbing, they have predetermined the revelation of God in which they will live.

We are blessed with the testimony of Scripture and the attestations of history that affirm the validity of these revelations. We need not rediscover them; they can be appropriated by faith. What we as individuals do need to do is to meet God! God has revealed everything about Himself that we will need to know to respond to Him in vital worship. His hand is outstretched in warm anticipation of a handshake. Reach out through the pages of this book and shake hands with God.

Judson Cornwall
4332 E. Shangri-la
Phoenix, AZ 85028

chapter one

ADAM COMPLETELY KNEW GOD

"...that they may know You, the only true God...."
(John 17:3)

Since the depth of our worship is always proportional to the extent of our revelation of God, Adam must have been the best worshipper of Jehovah the world has ever seen; no man has ever known God as well as Adam. Formed by the hand of God, made in the divine image, animated by the inbreathed Spirit of God, Adam had a tremendous commonality with God. In a very real sense, Adam was God's own son; therefore, there was no strangeness between them. As partakers of the same nature, they inherently understood one another and could perfectly respond to each other, so for Adam worship was extremely normal.

Even the most vivid imagination cannot grasp the ease with which Adam in his sinless state related to God. Adam worshipped without a sense of guilt, fear, anxiety, separation or strangeness. There was nothing to divert his attention, no self-will to divide his loyalties and no evil to dull his mind and diminish his spiritual appetite. Worship for Adam was as natural and uninhibited as nursing is to an infant.

In this innocent state, Adam maintained a strong sense of dignity and self-worth. He was unaware of any separation between himself and Jehovah, as most of us are. He fulfilled his purpose of being perfectly, and he felt very good about himself. He never acted in self-will, never violated a commitment and didn't even entertain thoughts that were inconsistent with the mind of God. Since Adam failed neither God nor himself, his self-image remained intact and untarnished. He could respond to God without self-recrimination. His talks with God, unlike ours, did not start with repentance. Adam could rejoice in God from the first moment of contact with Him, and with a perfect memory he began each communication with God right where the last had left off. Life was a constant progression with little need for repetition, for there was no subconscious repression of facts or feelings. Adam could deal with God in perfect honesty, for he had nothing to hide either from God or from himself.

Furthermore, Adam's undefiled relationship with God preserved a childlike trust. Adam could trust himself, so it was easy for him to trust God. Since everything that God said proved to be true, and every commitment made was fulfilled explicitly, trust in God was automatic and continuous. Actually, it was impossible for Adam to doubt God; there was absolutely no basis for mistrust either of God or of himself, for neither had ever failed the other. Since faith in another can rarely rise above our faith in ourselves, Adam had a distinct edge on all of us by having never broken faith with himself. He lived in moral perfection and found it very natural to trust a moral God. Every word spoken by God was accepted as absolute fact. Adam did not require repeated confirmations before he would trust God. That trust was automatic and absolute. It later took the full powers of Lucifer to instill a doubt about God in Adam's mind.

Adam Knew God Intimately

As incomprehensible as Adam's sinless state may be to those of us who have battled sin throughout our lives, this was only one factor in making Adam's worship so vital and unique. Equally important was his vast personal knowledge of God. Much of this knowledge was inherent. Adam was so like God that he could proceed from self-knowledge to knowledge of God. What God was, Adam was in miniature, so Adam had a foundation of the known from which to proceed into the unknown. He could sense God's nature by examining his own nature, and he could perceive God's feelings by extrapolating his own feelings. Not too unlike a couple in their fortieth year of marriage who can know what each other would do in a given situation, Adam knew God because of shared relationship. His intuitive powers were amazing.

But Adam's knowledge of God was further enhanced by his constant communication with God. God and Adam used to walk together in the garden of Eden and talk about the plants, animals, birds and fish. God was the only instructor Adam knew. Theirs was not a classroom setting; it was a Father-son walk in the garden. Adam learned about life from God, and in the process he learned about God.

What wonder and awe must have filled Adam's mind as he listened to God during those daily walks in the cool of the evening. What questions he must have saved up during the day, and what anticipation must have filled his heart as he awaited his opportunity to discuss them with God. Questions that send us to the *Encyclopedia Britannica* merely sent Adam to God. There is no scriptural evidence of these two ever discussing "spiritual" things; they talked about life as Adam was discovering it in Eden, and this seemed spiritual enough, since God was the source of all that life.

Imagine these two observing a sunset together. Adam would express his emotional reactions to the ever-changing beauty of the sky, while God would describe the properties of light and the laws of refraction that produce this daily phenomenon. Adam's wonder became God's delight, and God's wisdom became Adam's intrigue. Each benefited greatly from these times of talking together, and the pure enjoyment of it all was heightened because there was no one in existence to teach Adam to pray religious phrases when in God's presence.

It is unlikely that Adam had divided life into the sacred and the secular. He knew only one life, and that life was unequivocally wrapped up in God. Every time he talked to God, it was about God, and that is the very heart of worship, for worship speaks *to* God *about* God. Adam may have lacked stained-glass windows, pipe organs and robed choirs, but every time he talked with God was a worship session. He had no theological training, no music and no Bible, but he had God, and every response he made to God's voice was a worship response.

Both the Bible and history attest that many persons since Adam have heard the voice of God. But has anyone heard it so distinctly, so consistently, so conversationally, over so long a period of time as Adam? Some of the minor prophets devoted their mature years to proclaiming the message they heard from God; yet that message was shorter than any one evening's conversation between God and Adam. What heights of worship must have been reached in those unlimited talks!

Adam talked to God person to person as no one since has ever done, if for no other reason than the fact that before the creation of Eve, Adam had no one else with whom to communicate, and he had nothing to talk about but God and His works. When we briefly enjoy such communication with God, we call it worship.

Adam Lived in Covenant With God

Not only did Adam enjoy unlimited communication with God; he came to know a covenant-keeping God. Adam was not an indentured serf living on the master's estate, but a son living in a covenant relationship with his Father. Adam had the security of Eden, his own place, and he had the security of his relationship with God by virtue of Jehovah's covenant with him (see Gen. 1:26-28).

Adam had reason to embrace God's covenants, for every covenant God had made with nature was infallible. Didn't the sun rise every morning, and the moon rule over the stars every night? Adam never had to wonder what relationship he would have with God when he began his day, for he lived in a covenant relationship that was as unchanging as God is. God and Adam were far more than acquaintances; they were covenant friends whose relationship progressed but never regressed. It is likely that Adam's understanding of the depth of this covenant relationship unfolded as his understanding of God matured, but the covenant was complete the moment God spoke it.

Covenants, of course, involve commitments by two or more parties. God's contract with Adam demanded compliance with the stated conditions. Since this covenant was concerned with Adam's relationship with creation, with God and with himself, the conditions stated were threefold. In his relationship with creation, Adam was charged with leadership—"dominion"—over every living creature. As touching his relationship with God, Adam was pledged to obedience in the matter of eating the fruit of the tree of the knowledge of good and evil. Even in the matter of Adam's personhood, he was responsible to work in tending the garden. As long as Adam exerted leadership, obeyed God's commands and expressed himself in his work, he totally fulfilled his part in God's covenant.

Beyond this it was all up to God, and God never failed to meet His part of the contract. Adam related to God not as a petitioner but as a partner. He and God had entered into a contractual relationship, and they lived in that covenant bond very much as a husband and wife live together in a continuing covenant relationship.

What security and continuity this afforded Adam! Everything in his world belonged to him; nothing was withheld except the knowledge of evil. He lived perpetually in the knowledge of good and God. If worship is an expressed relationship between a person and God, Adam was a continual worshipper.

Adam Lived in Love With God

Adam came into this world with his arms locked around God in a love embrace. From his first breath, he knew that "God is love"; he did not have to read it in the Bible or hear it in a sermon. Adam knew a moral God whose very nature was loving, gentle, gracious and compassionate. It never entered Adam's mind that God might reject him, for the loving acceptance he had experienced became his expectation. His times of fellowship with God were used not so much to develop a loving relationship as to enjoy an existing relationship, for God and Adam had always been "in love." Furthermore, God was Adam's first love; there had been none before Him. With the innocence of childhood sweethearts who marry young, Adam never had to repress mental images of former love experiences. His was still a "first love," and it was all the more precious because of its purity.

When Eve first asked Adam what God was like, Adam's response must have been "God is love." Since worship is love responding to love, Adam was a great worshipper, and he likely introduced Eve to the worship of God.

Yes, Adam knew God far more intimately and loved God more perfectly than any one since the expulsion from Eden. Adam knew God in His perfect holiness, and he knew Him as the glorious light of all heaven and earth. God was not a distant creator but a constant companion. Those things that we tend to classify as "supernatural" were ordinary to Adam, for he knew by experience that everything God did was natural to Him. Creation and creator were so intertwined for Adam that life became one continuous response to God. Even breathing was almost worship, for Adam's breath had come from the mouth of God. Life and loving God were one and the same for Adam, and God loved it!

Adam Traded Relationship for Knowledge

But Satan despised this loving relationship. With all the subtlety he could muster, Satan in the image of Eden's serpent approached Eve and began a dialogue intended to discredit God and to create dissatisfaction in mankind.

Insisting that God was withholding vital information from them in not allowing them to see into the mystery of iniquity, Satan eventually got Adam and Eve to eat of the forbidden fruit. Adam allowed that over which he had been given dominion—both the serpent and Eve—to exercise dominion of him, and in doing so he violated the very first condition of his covenant with God. In eating of the fruit of the tree of the knowledge of good and evil, he violated the second condition. Adam got his own way and began a lifetime of learning about evil, but it cost him everything that God had given to him.

He was quickly expelled from Eden. His access to the tree of life was forever forfeited. His intimate contact with God was replaced with substitutionary sacrifices on a burning altar. Adam lost forever his wonderful state of sinlessness, and with that confiscation went his image of self-worth and dignity. He had disobeyed, violated a covenant and exercised self-will. Could he ever trust himself again? His childlike trust of God was now threatened by his manlike distrust of himself. He had yearned to know the mystery of evil, but he did not know that evil is not mentally comprehended—it is experientially appropriated. His desire to add to his realm of knowledge succeeded in exchanging knowledge of good for knowledge of evil, and Adam found it far more difficult to relate to a God who is inherently good.

The loud screaming of the voice of guilt made it more and more difficult for Adam to hear the voice of God. When he finally did discern God's voice, it was only to be corrected and then expelled from the garden. The covenant-keeping God had no choice but to fulfill the terms of the covenant in the event of disobedience. The loving embraces of acceptance were lost to Adam as he was driven both from the garden and from God's presence. No longer was God's voice to be heard in the cool of the day, nor was His wisdom available for the asking. Adam found himself separated from God, and he did not know how to handle it. A companionship he had enjoyed for all of his existence was now lost to him. It was worse than the death of a long-term marriage partner. In one sweep of divine justice Adam found himself deported from the only land he had ever known, separated from the source of his life, denied the fellowship and knowledge he had always enjoyed, and reduced to his own capacities. His labor as caretaker of the ground was now less fulfilling and rewarding than it was frustrating and exhausting, for God had cursed the earth as part of Adam's punishment. He now earned his living by the sweat of his brow.

None of us can truly empathize with Adam, for we were born in sin and grew up with iniquity, but Adam was plunged from innocence to sin in a moment of time. Like the stockbrokers in the late 1920s when the market crashed, all Adam could think of was "All is lost. Everything is gone!"

Adam's Sin Separated Mankind From God

As the prophet would later proclaim, "Your iniquities have separated you from your God; and your sins have hidden His face from you" (Is. 59:2). With this separation went a forfeited covenant, a cessation of revelation and a seeming inability to communicate to the children what Adam had learned about God, and worship became almost a lost art to mankind.

What price sin!—not only for Adam but for the entire human race, for Adam's forfeiture passed on to his progeny. His children never knew the relationship with God that he had enjoyed. God's voice was silenced; His companionship was forfeited; His love was virtually unknown; His covenants were forgotten. Even mankind's concepts of God's nature were distorted. God became an unknown quotient to most people, and they began to live as though there were no God.

So chapter 3 of the book of beginnings ends with the sad report that God "drove out the man; and He placed cherubim at the east of the garden of Eden, and a flaming sword which turned every way, to guard the way to the tree of life" (Gen. 3:24). The next chapter speaks of the birth of Adam's first son, Cain, and Eve's joyful exclamation "I have gotten a man from the Lord" (Gen. 4:1). Later she bore another son, whom they named Abel. This family became both the source and the object of Adam's fellowship and companionship. What he had lost in God, he sought to find in his family, but Adam soon learned that he had transmitted his sinful self-will to his sons. Cain's murder of Abel and God's expulsion of Cain reduced Adam to the solitude of his marriage until God mercifully gave them another son, Seth.

The chronicler has condensed the history of mankind from creation to the flood by revealing two separate streams of humanity springing from Adam. Through Cain's line we meet seven generations, and through

Seth's line we are introduced to the ten antediluvian patriarchs. That the progeny of Cain would precede the description of the line of Seth may simply acknowledge that Cain was the older son or it may imply that Adam's sinful nature was imputed far more powerfully than his spiritual nature.

In these genealogies there is an amazing similarity between the names given to the children, in the two lines, suggesting that the families remained in close enough proximity to influence one another in the choice of names. It is also interesting that, strange to say, civilization made far greater strides among those alienated from God than among those who were devoted to Him. It was Cain who built the first city, perhaps as a fort of defense against God's curse. The first poem came from the lips of the first bigamist, Lamech (in the sixth generation from Cain), and Lamech's sons were the first musicians and implement makers. The arts and sciences began with those who had rebelled against God, perhaps as a distraction of their souls from the emptiness they felt without God, and perhaps as a form of competition with the godly Sethites. Adam's first progeny excelled in knowledge to the exclusion of relationship with God, just as Adam had in the garden. How it must have wounded Adam to see his firstborn son producing generations of persons who were filling their lives with substitutes for God.

The godly branch of humanity that came through Adam's third son, Seth, is characterized as being as different from the Cain line as people coming from the same roots can be. Simplicity of life and devotedness to their God marked this second group, at least in their beginnings. Seth named his first son Enosh, which most lexicographers believe means "frailty" or "frail one." While the lineage of Cain was bolstering its strength to face the rigors of life, the beginning of Seth's lineage was given a name that would constantly remind all persons of the frailty of their mortal life. This does not necessarily indicate pessimism or discouragement; it is expressive of deep, unvarnished truth, for they recognized that man, apart from God, is hopelessly frail and weak.

The Beginning of Public Worship

The Scriptures follow the naming of Enosh with the statement "Then men began to call on the name of the Lord" (Gen. 4:26). By common consent, the lexicons interpret the expression *gara' beshem yahweh* to mean "use the name of Yahweh in worship." Obviously Adam had communicated a measure of truth about God to Seth, who communicated it to Enosh, and the three of them moved from private worship to public worship, for calling out or using God's name definitely implies public worship. The Sethites introduced public worship about the same time the Cainites were introducing poetry and music. The first bared their souls in calling upon the name of the Lord; the second soothed their souls with music and literature. The contrast is as vivid today as it was then. The Sethites wanted to be known as those whose hope was placed only in God. Adam's second lineage began well in humble public worship.

What follows the announcement of public worship is called "the book of the genealogy of Adam" or "the history of Adam" (Gen. 5:1), for this whole period of development of the line of godly men was Adam's history working itself out. The age was dominated by the spirit and influence of Adam. It is this group, not the other, that had the spirit of Adam, and this group alone became the ancestors of Abraham. This innocuous list of ten men is, for that season, the woman's seed. If during a millennium and a half these are the only names worthy of being handed down in the inspired Word of God, we do well to regard these men as deserving of an unusual measure of respect and renown. They were unquestionably patriarchs of the faith, but we must admit that, aside from Enoch, nothing is told us about them except that they lived lengthy lives, bore sons and daughters, and died. Nothing else they did is deemed worthy of mention in God's view. Ten men are mentioned, eight of whom would have known Adam personally, and their lives spanned from creation to 350 years beyond the flood, but except for the brief statement that ''Enoch walked with God; and was not, for God took him'' (Gen. 5:24), we know nothing about them until Noah.

It is never fair to argue from the silence of Scripture, but the condition of mankind at the time of Noah would indicate either a severe degeneration in the spiritual life of the Sethites or a prolific bearing of children by the Cainites—probably both. Adam's influence became less and less as his line grew larger and larger. He could give his children the history of his relationship with God, but he could not bring them into such a relationship for themselves. As all denominations have since discovered, the fervor and life-changing experiences of the founder diminish as each generation seeks to teach them to the next.

Since, according to the chronology given to us in Genesis 5, Adam died about 126 years before Noah's birth, Adam departed this earthly life with an awareness

27

that even among the godly there had come such a departure from God as to make the sin in Eden pale by comparison. Just as the effects of the tree of life eventually wore out in Adam's body, so the effects of the righteousness of God diminished in Adam's line as they found themselves cut off from the divine presence. Sin, not righteousness, prevailed. If God's promise of a deliverer coming through the seed of the woman was ever to be fulfilled, something needed to be done to curb the rapid rise of wickedness.

God's answer was to reveal Himself again, for God had not created mankind to be totally separated from Himself. Because of the darkness of man's mind and his disposition toward evil, God chose to unfold Himself in limited measure, wait until that revelation became a part of people's lives, then unfold more about Himself. The men to whom such impartations were given have become the heroes of our Bible, and their lives were radically affected by what they learned of God. Little by little, what Adam lost in God the saints have had restored to them so that God may be fully worshipped and enjoyed.

Obviously, for God to bring mankind back into intimate relationship with Himself, He must first bring them back into personal communication with Himself. But that task proved far more difficult than it would seem. For the thousand or more years between Adam and the birth of Noah, God sought communication with mankind, but there is no record of any of them actually hearing God's voice.

chapter two

NOAH MET
A SPEAKING GOD

"God...has...spoken to us...."
(Hebrews 1:1,2)

It is unfortunate that Noah is so inexorably connected with the ark and the flood that his personhood is often completely ignored. According to the biblical account, Noah was far more than a shipbuilder and a zoologist; he was the last of the ten antediluvian patriarchs of the Seth line, and he seems to have been the only one of them to hear the voice of God—after Adam's expulsion from Eden. Like modern religion, Noah had history, tradition, ritual and perhaps sacraments to assist him in reaching out to God, but these cannot be substituted for direct communication between God and men.

Since Noah was born about 1056 B.C. (according to the chronology of Genesis 5), he barely missed knowing Adam (who lived 930 years) and Seth, but it is highly probable that Lamech, Noah's father, knew Adam. Any teaching, tradition, ritual or sacrament that Adam desired to hand down was in only the second generation at the time of the flood.

Noah's Contemporaries

Except for Enoch, whom God translated at age 365, all of these Sethite patriarchs lived nine hundred or more years, so six of them were still living when Noah was born, and Seth's death preceded Noah's birth by only fourteen years. What a power for godliness it should have been to have these seven patriarch believers living simultaneously and encouraging one another for such long periods of time. But what should have been and what actually happened are poles apart. Quite obviously, godly lineage does not always produce godly families. The best of men lived in the worst of times and seemed unable to prevent or override the wickedness of their own generations. Speaking of this patriarchal lineage listed in Genesis 5, James Hastings says in *The Speaker's Bible*, ''It is a monotonous chronicle of nobodies. One after another they deploy before us, a moment visible, and then gone forever. The only memorial they have left us is that they were born and begat children and died.''

Far from producing righteousness on the earth, these men, at best, lived in contrast to the rest of their world, but they did not seem to condemn or counter the flagrant godlessness that surrounded them. In contrast to these seven venerable old men were the ''giants'' (Hebrew *Nephilim*) who seemed to be the offspring of intermarriage between the unbelieving Cainite men and the believing Sethite women. History speaks of these as marauding nomads, as men of a violent, overbearing, lawless character, roving from place to place in quest of plunder, attacking both property and lives. They broke off the restraints of religion and settled in such lustful living as to become persons of reckless ferocity who spread carnage far and wide. Their monstrous strength and terror became so well known that they were acclaimed as heroes who would, in times to come, be exalted by different nations, under various names, as the demigods of pagan mythology.

It is bad enough when evil men are honored in spite of their wickedness, but when men are honored for their wickedness, and the vilest men are exalted, what hope can there be for civilization? God's appraisal of the moral condition of the earth in the days of Noah is expressed in the statement "The Lord saw that the wickedness of man was great in the earth, and that every intent of the thoughts of his heart was only evil continually" (Gen. 6:5). All of the wrong deeds sprang from the wrong desires. The corruption in the earth sprang from the moral corruption of humanity's nature. Principles were so perverted that people did evil not only through carelessness but through design. The historian adds, "The earth also was corrupt before God, and the earth was filled with violence" (Gen. 6:11). The Hebrew word for violence is *chamas*, which basically means "high-handed dealing; violating the rights of others," and the construction of this verse in its original language implies a fantastic excess of depravity.

So severe was the unbridled wickedness that "the Lord was sorry that He had made man on the earth, and He was grieved in His heart" (Gen. 6:6). Sin is not only disastrous to mankind; it is grievous to God. The violent sin in Noah's time was so lamentable to God that He "repented" (KJV) or "was sorry" (NKJV) that He had made man (v. 7). What disappointment this depravity produced in God; but although it is recorded that God was sorry that He made man, nowhere do the Scriptures say that He has ever been sorry He redeemed man. Hallelujah!

Quite obviously Noah came onto the pages of history at a dark and dismal time. The account of wickedness, violation of the rights of others, robbery and violence, and the making of heroes of those who lived such lawless lives sounds strangely familiar. These are the themes of so many of our current movies, and we Americans seem to enjoy making heroes of the lawless ones who live and act as the Nephilim of Noah's day. But then, Jesus warned us that "as the days of Noah were, so also will the coming of the Son of Man be" (Matt. 24:37). Is it possible that the crime, lawlessness, ungodliness, violence and terror of our generation equal the iniquity of Noah's day? Does the influence of the godless overpower the influence of the godly? If so, beware, for God has not changed His attitude toward sin.

Noah's Birth

In the midst of this darkness came the tenth in the line of Adam, and his birth is announced in such a way as to make it evident that this child came at a crucial time with a critical mission. The stereotyped expression "lived [years] and begot [name]" used in chapter 5 is sidestepped. Genesis 5:28 says, "Lamech lived one hundred and eighty-two years, and begot a son." With a measure of formality, Moses added, "And he called his name Noah." Finally, the reason for giving this name is mentioned: "This one will comfort us."

Numerous ancient books, referred to as the Dead Sea Scrolls, have been discovered since 1945. One of them, the *Ethiopic Enoch*, describes the newborn Noah as a wonder child. As the story goes, Lamech, suspecting

that he might be the father of an intrusive angel, con-
sulted his father, Methuselah, who in turn went to the
"the ends of the earth" to consult his father, Enoch.
Enoch confirmed that Noah was indeed Lamech's son,
and that God would do "a new thing on the earth" in
Noah's day. Essentially the same story appears in the
Genesis Apocryphon from Qumran and in fragments
from Cave Four, one of which even gives the baby's
weight. While these are obviously not a part of the inspired Scriptures, they are interesting, and they shed
some light upon the high veneration in which Noah was
held by early civilization.

Noah's name is associated with rest, although the actual etymology of the name is uncertain. *Noah* comes
from an entirely different word from *nuach*, "to rest,"
but the two words sound alike, and Lamech was probably making a play on words. Lamech gave as his reason
for choosing the name, "This one will comfort us concerning our work and the toil of our hands, because of
the ground which the Lord has cursed" (Gen. 5:29).
By the spirit of prophecy, Lamech, like other godly
patriarchs, sensed that in an unusual way this one would
bring comfort or rest to the troubled race.

Apparently the misery of work and of the "toil of
the hands" was beginning to weigh heavily upon men.
Life had become a ceaseless round of unrelieved toil,
and men longed for deliverance, or at least for comfort
under the burden. Although they understood that their
wretchedness was the result of the curse which had been
pronounced upon the ground because of sin, there is
little evidence that they were seeking to live sinlessly.
They merely wanted someone to give them relief and
comfort them in their sorrows.

Expectations for Noah

Regardless of the outstanding traits his parents saw in him, what was expected of Noah must have been a towering burden. He saw not only the extreme contrast between the righteousness of a few and the ungodliness of the many, but, most likely, he was told repeatedly what his name stood for and the exorbitant expectations his parents had set for him. To be seen as the deliverer from the oppression of the curse that God Himself had placed upon man would be an unbearable burden for Noah. Much later in Israel's history Moses lived with this same pressure of knowing that he was to be a deliverer, but not knowing how to fulfill that commission.

Lamech may have taken comfort in the coming of Noah, but this son must have had difficulty trying to be normal in the midst of such abnormally high hopes. Regardless of the truth of Lamech's prophecy, Noah was powerless to fulfill his parents' expectations, for prophetic insight and power to perform are not synonymous, nor necessarily consecutive.

The more godly Noah's life, the more he was rejected by his godless peers and hated by his generation; by both his life and his preaching he condemned the world. It is a fact of life: anyone chosen by God for a special task will know great loneliness.

Noah lived for five hundred years, and, although he walked with God and lived righteously, he did not see any alleviation of mankind's suffering. We now know that it was not the purpose of God to remove the curse from the earth—God had purposed to remove cursed man from the earth! But Noah did not have this perspective which is given to us by hindsight. Noah eventually learned that God sometimes delivers His people from the circumstance, and sometimes in the midst of the circumstance. Noah's peers expected him to solve the crisis, but God merely expected him to survive in the midst of that crisis.

Perhaps it was this pressure to perform, or maybe it was the vexation of the open lawlessness around him, that drove Noah to take a meditative walk in the countryside. Despondent enough to walk with bowed head, Noah was startled to hear a voice proclaim, "I will destroy man whom I have created from the face of the earth...for I am sorry that I have made them" (Gen. 6:7). I can imagine that Noah turned in a complete circle. Even though he didn't see anyone, the voice was unmistakably real. It couldn't have come from within himself, for Noah had never considered such an outlandish thought, nor would he ever claim to have created man. "Whom I have created"—this must be God Himself speaking, Noah thought.

Instinctively Noah looked upward. As God's eyes swept once again over the earth, viewing the depravity of mankind, He found Himself looking into the eyes of an upturned face. Noah had heard God's voice and was responding!

NH Equals HN

Two pairs of eyes met on that summer afternoon. God looked deep into the soul of the one man in over a thousand years who had responded to His voice, and Noah looked into the eyes of a grieved God; and "Noah found grace in the eyes of the Lord" (Gen. 6:8).

Only the consonants were written in the early Hebrew language. Accordingly, the Hebrew word that we have translated "grace" is spelled *HN*—while Noah's name is *NH*. Grace is *Noah* spelled backwards. Grace was a mirror image of Noah: NH equals HN.

As Noah looked at his decadent generation, he found something of himself in everyone he saw. He recognized that "the heart is deceitful above all things, and desperately wicked; who can know it?" (Jer. 17:9). When reading the story of Noah, we must remind ourselves that it was a disciplined life, not dissimilar desires, that made Noah different from his contemporaries, for Noah was capable of everything he saw in others. Furthermore, by this time in his life—for by now he was over five hundred years old—Noah knew that he was not the deliverer his father had expected. It is likely that he carried a debilitated self-image.

When he looked around him, Noah saw depravity; when he looked inward, he saw despondency; but when God's voice taught him to look upward, he saw grace. Gazing into God's eyes, Noah saw himself reflected as just the opposite of his self-image. He saw grace instead of disgrace, acceptance instead of rejection, love instead of hate, and approval instead of disapproval. What a pleasant surprise it must have been to discover that God saw him as so much better than he saw himself!

In this first occurrence of the word "grace" in the Bible, we learn that grace comes by beholding, not merely by believing. Just as our eyes do not reach out to an object, but the light from that object reaches into the eyes, so we cannot reach out to lay hold upon grace; grace reaches out to lay hold upon us as we behold the face of God. Paul summarized this in writing, "But we all, with unveiled face, beholding as in a mirror the glory of the Lord, are being transformed into the same image from glory to glory, just as by the Spirit of the

Lord'' (2 Cor. 3:18). Beholding, we are changed. When Noah saw himself mirrored in the eyes of God, he realized that he was the object of God's grace rather than a sharer in man's disgrace. It was as though God put on His ''grace glasses'' every time Noah looked up. By faith Noah saw not only God; he saw himself as God saw him, and because he was willing to accept what he saw in God's eyes beyond what he saw in his own life, Noah came back to the self-image that Adam had enjoyed before the fall. Grace restored what sin had stolen, and it still does.

How we need to see ourselves as God sees us! Far too frequently we carry damagingly unreal self-images produced by guilt. We tend to visualize our limitations instead of God's greatness in us, and we magnify our failures instead of God's ability to make even these ''things work together for good.'' When we minimize what God has said about us, we reject the high positions He has given to us because we look at ourselves directly instead of in the mirror of God's eyes. When coming to God's Word, which James calls a ''mirror,'' we can see either our imperfections, as the Old Testament priests did in the laver, or we can see divine grace made available to us, and appropriate it for our lives. The cliche ''What you see is what you get'' may well be adapted to read ''What you see is what you become,'' for, as Jeremiah cried out, ''Mine eye affecteth mine heart'' (Lam. 3:51, KJV).

Noah, the ''Graced Man''

Noah was a very good man, but he was no better than the grace of God made him. As Paul later testified, ''But by the grace of God I am what I am, and His grace toward me was not in vain; but I labored more

37

abundantly than they all, yet not I, but the grace of God which was with me'' (1 Cor. 15:10). Look at the scriptural record of what God's grace managed to effect in Noah.

God's grace made Noah ''a just man'' according to Genesis 6:9. The Hebrew word for ''just'' is in our English alphabet *tsaddiq*, a word commonly used to indicate that someone conforms to a standard. Noah conformed to the divine standard and therefore met God's approval. While this does not imply perfection on Noah's part, it does imply that those things that God desired of mankind were present in Noah. Primarily, God desired man to believe Him and His promise of help through the seed of the woman, and Noah did this and was declared righteous in God's sight (see Gen. 3:15).

This grace that Noah saw in the eyes of the Lord made Noah a man ''perfect in his generations'' (Gen. 6:9). Grace made Noah blameless or faultless among his contemporaries. The Hebrew word used for ''perfect'' is *tamim*, which comes from a root that means ''complete.'' Noah lived a well-rounded complete life. He was not merely a mystic; he was a balanced man who lived life to the fullest extent. Grace is never intended to make us weird; it comes to make us complete. Jesus said, ''I have come that they may have life, and that they may have it more abundantly'' (John 10:10). God's goodness has been made available to us to bring us into life, more life and abundant life. Noah was perfect in life, and because of that he stood high above his contemporaries, for they lacked the grace that completes one's life.

God's grace also made Noah a man who ''walked with

God'' (Gen. 6:9). The Hebrew signifies "to walk about," and the preposition *'eth* is used with this word only in reference to Enoch and Noah. These two men walked in the most intimate communion with God. While some feel that God appeared in human form—a theophanic manifestation—enabling Noah quite literally to walk with God, it is far more likely that this is a figurative expression. Noah remained conscious of the nearness of the almighty God and walked as the thought of that presence determined. The type of walking that Noah did is still possible for any of us, for the Word teaches us to "walk in the Spirit," to be "led by the Spirit" and to "live in the Spirit" (Gal. 5:16,18,25).

The great New Testament list of the heroes of faith includes Noah and says, "By faith Noah, being divinely warned of things not yet seen, moved with godly fear, prepared an ark for the saving of his household, by which he condemned the world and became heir of the righteousness which is according to faith" (Heb. 11:7). The writer of the book of Hebrews pointed out seven things that grace produced in Noah. He was "warned of God"; was informed of "things not yet seen"; was "moved with fear" [Rotherham, "filled with reverence"]; "prepared an ark"; "saved his house"; "condemned the world"; "became heir of the righteousness...according to faith."

All of this was at a time of depravity and gross departure from God. As Matthew Henry long ago wrote, "It is easy to be religious when religion is in fashion; but it is evidence of strong faith and resolution to swim against the stream, and to appear for God, when no one else appears for Him: Noah did so."

Noah could hardly have stepped into history at a worse

time, but because he elected to look at God rather than at contemporary life, he lived righteously, perfectly and full of faith, in a walk with God that preserved both him and his family in the time of disastrous judgment. It was his position not in history but in the heart of God that made the difference. He believed God, not the apparent facts.

The formula that made such a difference in the life of Noah was *NH* equals *HN*. Noah, mirrored in God's eyes, equals grace. The same formula will work for any Christian. When you see yourself in God's eyes and believe what you see, it makes such grace available to you as to transform you from the ordinary to the extraordinary, from carnality to spirituality, from failure to success, and from passivity to activity.

Like the children of Israel bitten by serpents who were commanded to look at the brazen serpent and live, we need to regain the upward look. We have passed through too lengthy a season of introspection. We have examined ourselves in every possible way, but we have been unable to effect radical changes. We need to gaze into God's realm until we catch a glimpse of God's face turned toward us in gracious love and compassion, and then we should fix our eyes upon Jesus until His grace makes us into His own image here in this world.

Noah and God's Voice

What a treasure Noah found when he looked into God's face; but it would never have happened if he hadn't heard the plaintive voice of God. Adam enjoyed divine grace as long as he had unrestricted communication with God; but once Adam was expelled from the garden, that communication seems to have ceased. The last recorded communication between God and humanity was God's judgment of Cain for murdering his brother Abel (see Gen. 4:6 ff.). Not once during the thousand years between Adam and Noah does the Genesis record refer to God speaking to anyone on this earth. It does not even say that He spoke to Enoch, who "walked with God."

What a long silence! We can only speculate as to what part this silence played in humanity's severe declension from the faith. Would man have so departed from God if he had been talking with God? The New Testament teaches us that "the goodness of God leads you to repentance" (Rom. 2:4), but do we actually see God's goodness when divine communication has been severed? These succeeding generations had history, tradition and a few godly examples, but they lacked a fresh revelation of and from God.

Moral depravity is the tangible result of not hearing from God, for if we don't hear God's voice we will hear and respond to other voices, and neither our own inner voices nor the outer voices of the demonic realm direct us into righteousness and holiness. Mankind, untutored and undirected by God, descends to the lowest level of degradation; at least that is the history lesson before us, for God observed that "every intent of the thoughts of [man's] heart was only evil continually" (Gen. 6:5). This was also the position Paul took in the beginning of his letter to the Romans where he argued that God revealed Himself to mankind—He spoke to us—but we suppressed the truth, were unthankful and unresponsive and "exchanged the truth of God for the lie, and worshipped and served the creature rather than the Creator, who is blessed forever. Amen. For this reason God gave them up to vile passions" (see Rom. 1:18-32).

41

Paul's argument that God is speaking to men makes one wonder if this millennium of noncommunication from God was because God had ceased to speak, or because man had ceased to listen. Would God have been justified in destroying a race of people who had never been given an opportunity to hear? Perhaps men worked so hard trying to overcome the result of God's curse that they did not listen to the voice of the One who had cursed the earth in the first place.

Divine Communication Is Necessary

At the very end of the Seth patriarchal line, Noah heard the voice of God. Did he hear God's voice because he was the last in the line, or did he become the last in his line because he, among all of his peers, heard God's voice? The prophet Amos declared, "Surely the Lord God does nothing, unless He reveals His secret to His servants the prophets" (Amos 3:7). If this principle is inviolate, and it certainly seems to be, then God could not judge sinning people until He could find one person who would listen to Him describe how He felt and what He purposed to do. When Noah began to discern God's voice, the first thing that God told him was "My Spirit shall not strive with man forever, for he is indeed flesh; yet his days shall be one hundred and twenty years" (Gen. 6:3). God actually told Noah how much longer man would live on the earth, and 120 years later the flood came. For that 120 years Noah became a "preacher of righteousness" (2 Pet. 2:5) to his generation, but only his family responded. If people will not hear God, they will not hear God's preacher, as thousands of clergymen in our generation can attest.

Noah not only preached righteousness; he demonstrated it. In contrast to his peers, Noah was a shining

42

light of godliness, and personal communion with God was the taproot of this outstandingly good life. He could please God because he knew what God desired. He became a man of faith because he listened to God's voice, for "faith comes by hearing, and hearing by the word of God" (Rom. 10:17). The more Noah heard from God, the more his faith matured and the more righteous his life became.

Somehow our generation thinks that God has ceased speaking or that if He were to speak, He would talk theology. But God did not discuss theological concepts with Noah; He shared His thoughts, feelings and plans with him. God communicated dimensions, material lists and construction details for the ark, and this communication was not vague but very specific. We need to know that God can communicate on any subject and can counsel us in every avenue of life if we will but develop a listening ear and believe what He is saying.

The Genesis account of God's speaking to Noah shows that this communication was basically a revelation of God's person. To begin with, God let Noah see mankind's wickedness from the divine perspective by telling Noah what He saw (Gen. 6:5). Then God let Noah feel with His feelings by telling Noah that He was sorry—"repented"—He had made man (Gen. 6:6). It must have been quite a shock to Noah to see things God's way and to know how God was feeling about what He saw, for it was certainly different from anything he had heard the other patriarchs talk about.

Once Noah could understand Jehovah's feelings, God let him in on the divine plans for destroying the earth (Gen. 6:13), and then God clearly instructed him in the preparation of an ark that would preserve him and his family, plus the animals and birds (Gen. 6:14 ff.). True victorious living is knowing what God is doing, and doing it with Him. Noah excelled in this because his communication channel was distinct and clear—so clear, in fact, that he could not be passive. He obeyed God perfectly, for we read, "Noah did according to all that the Lord commanded him" (Gen. 7:5). None is more active in the service of God than the one who hears the voice of God clearly.

Divine Communication Is Available

If Noah could be delivered by listening to the voice of God and obeying it, so can we! What Adam forfeited, Noah found! Walking and talking with God have been restored to humanity. We have the voice of the Lord recorded in the Bible. We have God's voice being communicated through His anointed servants and prophets. We are assured that "God...has in these last days spoken to us by His Son" (Heb. 1:1, 2), and we have the voice of the Spirit speaking within our spirits. No generation in the history of the world has had God's voice as available as has this generation, but does our obedience match that availability? The level of holiness in the lives of the very ones who claim to have heard God's voice looks minute in comparison with the communication received.

Perhaps our generation is more concerned with the retransmission of God's voice than with responding to that voice. We love to give prophetic utterances declaring that "this is the voice of God," but could God get us to build an ark on the basis of such communication? Pastors spend hours in the preparation and delivery of sermons that are declared to be "the word of God," but how seldom those sermons affect behavior outside the church building. We enthusiastically applaud what we hear as a manifestation of God's voice; and we emotionally sing songs of praise to His name; but God's voice is meant to direct and guide, not merely to excite. If we do not obey a communication from God, we actually are rebels.

It could be that we are not so much protesting God's voice as pretending that we hear it. Like persons with a hearing disability who pretend to understand the conversation but who are betrayed by their remarks, religion has a way of projecting that it is hearing the voice of God when in fact it has but a record of what was heard in the past. Unfortunately, however, when religion loses its communication with God it degenerates into ritual, substitutes form for fellowship and talking to men for talking with God. How often have our prayer meetings been reduced to talking to one another about our problems and anxieties instead of talking with God. Even public praying is more likely to be pharisaical talking to the congregation than humble communication with God. Some of the best sermons I have preached have been masked as prayers to God—but everyone knows that God does not need to be preached to.

Just like our personal relationships, our relationship with God degenerates when communication breaks down. When we no longer talk to Him we soon cease to walk with Him; and what is true individually is equally true collectively. The historical record of what God has said in the past is not in itself sufficient to keep us in a vital, current relationship with God. The great truths that God spoke into the heart of a denomination's founder never inspire the second generation as they did the founder, and by the time those truths are taught to the third and fourth generations they usually have been reduced to cold logic and dogma.

Organized religion seems to handle divine communication in this manner: The first generation embraces it; the second generation codifies it; the third generation modifies it; and the fourth generation erases it. Children often play a game called "pass it on"—one person whispers a simple statement into the ear of the next. The "secret" is passed around the room and eventually repeated aloud by the last person. Usually the final word bears little or no resemblance to what the first person said. That same process often happens to inspired truth that is merely "passed on"; it becomes deceptively distorted.

We all need more than truth that has been communicated; we need the communication of the truth. Men need to hear from God! If we will but listen and learn, respond and obey, we will realize that walking and talking with God have, indeed, been restored to mankind for all of time and eternity!

Divine Communication Induces Worship

God's communication with Noah brought him into a full worship response to God. After the flood waters receded and Noah was released from the ark, "Noah built an altar to the Lord, and took of every clean animal and of every clean bird, and offered burnt offerings on the altar" (Gen. 8:20). When setting foot upon a purged earth Noah's first action was to worship the Lord.

And what worship he offered! In view of the fact that he had but seven pairs of clean animals and birds with which to fill the world, taking one of each to offer to God as a burnt offering was indeed magnanimous. When has a more liberal offering been given to God: one-seventh of every living, acceptable species? But then when has a man had as much reason for gratitude and thanksgiving? All around him Noah saw signs of rejuvenation; etched deeply in his present memory was the most awful catastrophe in the annals of mankind; above him the true and faithful Lord God was accepting the ascending fragrance of this sacrifice. His praise was very up to date.

God's response to this offering was twofold. "And the Lord smelled a soothing aroma. Then the Lord said..." (Gen. 8:21).

God smelled, and God spoke. The ascending smoke from Noah's altar was completely acceptable to God. It was "a sweet savor" (KJV). The Hebrew word for this statement comes from *nuach*, "to rest," and it is the word Noah's father used when giving a reason for naming his son Noah. What the earthly father had prophesied concerning his son, the heavenly Father proclaimed as accomplished. The meaning of this phrase is that the sacrifice was as pleasingly acceptable to God as refreshing odors are pleasant to the senses of a man or woman. It was far more than the ascending smoke that gave pleasure to Jehovah; it was the worshipping man on the chastened earth that so delighted God. Noah was not bitter at God—he blessed the Lord with worship!

Worship Induces Divine Communication

As God received Noah's worship, He resumed communication with Noah by blessing both him and his sons and by assuring him that this deluge would never be repeated. Worship renews communication with God, and He is most likely to speak to us as we worship Him. God delights in speaking to His people, but the great whirl of life's activity often dulls our consciousness of His voice. During worship, our minds are quieted, our activities are centered upon God and our spiritual sensitivity is heightened. Communication with God is vital to worship, for worship is the expression of our deepest attitudes of love and adoration. As I have so often said and written, "Worship is love responding to love; or, better yet, worship is two lovers responding to each other." How can this be successfully executed without communication? Worship must be more than a person talking to his God, for worship is a dialogue, not a monologue. Worship is bilateral, not unilateral. When an individual and his or her God flow loving feelings and positive attitudes to one another, a worship experience occurs. Noah could worship because he had learned two-way communication with Jehovah!

If Noah could become a worshipper by listening and responding to the voice of God, so can we! God is a superb teacher! He delights in giving "on-the-job training," and He turns a religious chore into an exchange of love. In spite of our generation with all of its permissiveness and self-centeredness, the person who looks to God's face and listens to His voice can become an accepted worshipper who finds favor with God, just as Noah did.

Adam knew God completely but lost the source of that knowledge through his sin; Noah began to gain some of that same knowledge through communication with God. God is a self-revealing God who desires that mankind know Him fully.

It is true that everything Adam lost, God has restored to us, but this restoration has come one factor at a time. Each person through whom God restored something that had been lost was already a possessor of what had been regained through others, for the knowledge of God comes cumulatively, as Isaiah said: "The word of the Lord was to them, 'Precept upon precept, precept upon precept, line upon line, line upon line, here a little, there a little' " (Is. 28:13).

Noah met a speaking God; the final communication God shared with him was a covenant never again to destroy the earth with water, and He set the rainbow as the visible sign of that covenant. In doing so, God was already beginning to reveal another facet of His nature to Noah. We do not know whether or not Noah actually grasped it, but when Abraham entered into communication with God, he met a covenant-keeping God.

chapter three

ABRAHAM MET A COVENANT-KEEPING GOD

"For our God is a consuming fire."
(Hebrews 12:29)

By coming into communication with a speaking God, Noah was able to save his entire household. From the first day that Noah recognized God's voice until God made a rudimentary covenant with him, everything God said to Noah was directed at a specific need in Noah's life. God spoke of the need to separate himself from the loathsome wickedness of that generation, and Noah did so by looking into God's face and finding grace. God also spoke of the need to escape the divine judgment that was about to be unleashed upon an idolatrous world, and Noah, following God's instructions, built an ark in which he, his family and selected animals survived. After the flood was over, God spoke of the need to repopulate the earth, and Noah became a farmer as well as a husbandman.

As long as God's communication related to a need in Noah's life, Noah instantly responded and obeyed, but after God pledged that He would never again destroy the earth by water, there is no further scriptural record of communication between Noah and God. Once Noah's known needs were met, it is possible that he no longer felt an urgency to communicate with God, for he was doing the last thing that God told him to do—"Be fruitful and multiply, and fill the earth" (Gen. 9:1). I realize that this is argued from the silence of Scripture, but it is supported by human nature, for most persons who enter into an intimate relationship with God do so out of personal need. Once those needs have been satisfied they cease walking and talking with God; instead they start reminiscing and talking about Him.

This may explain the 365 years of complete silence between God and men from the time of Noah to the days of Abraham. An emergency had been met with divine instruction, and perhaps Noah then chose not to bother God any further. The revelation that God delighted in communicating with men had not yet been appropriated. When mankind ceased speaking with God, they began to form their own concepts about God, so that by the time God's voice was heard by Abraham, the Chaldeans were deeply involved in idolatry. It is consistent in life that our concepts control our conduct, and the stronger the concept, the more rapid the change. Whereas before the flood it took men a thousand years to degenerate spiritually, after the flood they did it in one-third the time.

Noah had learned to relate to a God of the present, but he had no concept of a continuing relationship with God into the future. God had to look for another person who could accept the Noahian revelation as a starting point and move into a new discovery in the nature of God.

Abraham Heard God's Voice

After a period of time, God heard a response to His persistent calls. In Ur, the capital city of the idolatrous Chaldeans, a man, named Abram by his father but later renamed Abraham by God, answered a deep inner calling and discovered that Jehovah was speaking to him. Abraham, as he is known throughout the Bible after Genesis 16, was the tenth generation from Noah through Shem's lineage, just as Noah had been the tenth generation from Adam through Seth; and, like Noah, Abraham seemed able to discern the explicit voice of God very accurately.

How Abraham stepped into Noah's revelation that God was a speaking God is not recorded, but he did, and the first thing God instructed Abraham to do was "Get out of your country, from your kindred and from your father's house, to a land that I will show you" (Gen. 12:1). With this came the promise to make him into a great nation, to make his name great, to make him a blessing to all the families of the earth, and to curse all who cursed him (vv. 2,3) It was a tempting promise aimed at getting Abraham out of Ur—it was the carrot to move the donkey—and Abraham obeyed and left Ur. But when famine swept the area where he was dwelling, he took his wife, Sarah, and went to Egypt, where God miraculously preserved them in spite of their deceitfulness: they called Sarah Abraham's sister rather than his wife.

Thrust out of Egypt by Pharaoh, Abraham and Sarah returned to the land into which God had originally led them. God greatly prospered Abraham, offering him additional promises to keep him in the land. This time

Jehovah promised him all the land he could see and pledged that his descendants would be as numerous as the dust of the earth (see Gen. 13:14-17).

The promises made to Abraham, unlike the covenantal promise made to Noah, were conditional. The first promise demanded separation—"Get out of your country, from your kindred and from your father's house" (Gen. 12:1); the second promise demanded activation— "Arise, walk in the land through its length and its width, for I give it to you" (Gen. 13:17). Abraham was being stretched to reach into the future with his faith, whereas the promises made to Noah had mostly involved the present.

God did not make Abraham continue to live on intangible faith; He confirmed His promises to Abraham in at least three distinct ways. First, His protection in Egypt when He kept Sarah as Abraham's wife in spite of Pharaoh's attempt to take her as his own wife, was distinct evidence that the promise of future blessing was backed up with divine performance in the present (see Gen. 12:11-20). Second, His marvelous defeat of the three kings who had captured Sodom and Gomorrah and taken Lot, Abraham's nephew, with them, displayed His power to fulfill any promise (see Gen. 14:14-16). Third, the blessing of Melchizedek, king of Salem, was a prophetic confirmation of what God had earlier spoken to Abraham (see Gen. 14:17-20).

Promises Precede Covenants

God delights in giving us sufficient promises to get us out of our idolatrous realm and additional promises to entice us to remain in the provision He has made for us. He further enjoys demonstrating His promises to us through interventions in our lives, displays of power on our behalf and confirming ministries through the body of Christ. Many speak of walking in "blind faith," but I believe it more appropriate to speak of walking in "illuminating faith," for God loves to become light in our dark places.

God consistently confirms His promises to us and performs His promises for us, and He progressively increases those promises until we are able to enter into a covenant relationship with Him. In a sense we could say that responding to God's promises builds a "credit rating" which is checked before a covenant is offered. We must learn to be faithful in little before we will be trusted to be faithful in much. By watching how we handle the promises, God determines whom to bring into covenants. God does not want to enter into covenant relationships with vacillating persons, so He checks our consistency by observing how we keep the conditions of His simple promises to us.

There are, of course, distinct differences between a mere promise and a binding covenant. A promise is unilateral, while a covenant is bilateral. A promise is a commitment, but a covenant is a contract. Furthermore, God's promises are usually limited to time, while His covenants are eternal. Perhaps we could say that a promise is like an engagement, while a covenant is like a marriage. Unquestionably, there is more force in a covenant than in a mere promise. This may be why the Bible, while containing hundreds of promises, lists only seven major covenants that God made with men.

Principal Elements of Covenants

At least in Abraham's case, God's promises were intended to prepare him to enter into an eternal covenant with his God. Since the concept of covenants predates even Abraham's day, this would pose no problem for Abraham, for the Old Testament seems to accommodate the principal covenant elements that were common at that time.

The Hebrew word for "covenant" is *berith*, which has two shades of meaning. Usually it referred to a solemn mutual agreement; but it also meant a command; instead of an obligation voluntarily assumed, it was an obligation that has been imposed by a superior upon an inferior. For example, a conqueror might force a nation into a covenant by assessing tribute and conditions for continued peace. This shade of meaning is never applicable to God's covenants with mankind, for God desires to be served not out of compulsion but out of love.

In Abraham's day the principal elements in a covenant between men seem to have been: a statement of the terms agreed upon; an oath by each party to observe the terms, God being witness of the oath; and a curse invoked by each upon himself in case of a violation of the agreement. There was also a formal ratification of the covenant by some solemn external act such as the drinking of one another's blood, the offering of animals in "cutting covenant," feasting together (often on these sacrificial animals) or partaking of salt from one another's swords—the "covenant of salt."

The significant elements in a covenant between a superior and an inferior are best demonstrated by looking at discovered Hittite covenant treaties. The Hittite emperor always began by introducing himself and recalling his special favors toward the vassal. This unearned royal kindness called for one or two responses by the vassal: either the free pledge of loyalty and fidelity, which included an acceptance of certain duties, or the willful rejection of the emperor's kindness, which led to open rebellion against him.

Fidelity would maintain a proffered treaty and guarantee the state's continued favor, while infidelity to the treaty relationship would prompt curses and retribution. Many scholars see a great correspondence between the Mosaic covenant and the Hittite covenants.

Divine Covenants

Looking beyond secular history as the archaeologists have revealed it, the Bible shows the principal elements in a divine covenant between God and men to be similar to the historic documents, but far more solemn. In the Scriptures, God, the superior, always takes the initiative in establishing a divine covenant, but it is nonetheless regarded as a mutual agreement. God makes certain promises in conjunction with His commands, and when a person agrees to keep those commands, the covenant is "cut," for the promises in the covenant are conditioned on human obedience. Fundamentally, the covenant of God with men is a divine ordinance. It has signs and pledges on God's part, and it also has promises for human obedience and penalties for disobedience. This ordinance must be accepted by mankind before it is valid, for God is not forcing His will upon vassals; He is offering a covenant to His friends.

When we speak of divine covenants we generally think of the seven basic Bible covenants: the Adamic or Edenic covenant; the Noahian covenant; the Abrahamic covenant; the Mosaic or Sinaitic covenant; the Levitical covenant; the Davidic covenant; and the new covenant or the blood covenant. There are several lesser covenants, but these, such as the covenants of Hezekiah in his reforms, of Ezra in rebuilding the temple and of Nehemiah in rebuilding Jerusalem, were initiated by men with God and cannot accurately be designated as divine covenants.

Essentially, the purpose of God's covenants was to undergird His promises with a pledge that would provide faith and continuity in His people's relationship to Himself. These covenants unfolded something of the eternity of God's Word, and they brought a security to those who entered into the covenant with God. These covenants were never viewed as fearsome; they were amicable, for friendship is implied in all the covenants God made with mankind.

The Noahian covenant, which preceded the Abrahamic covenant by nearly four hundred years, actually was little more than a reaffirmation of God's covenant to Adam. Noah was challenged to "be fruitful and multiply, and fill the earth" (Gen. 9:1) and to have dominion over animals, birds and fish (Gen. 9:2), and he was assured that seedtime and harvest would not fail (Gen. 8:22), which sounds very much like a replay of Genesis 1. God's pledge never again to destroy the world by water was the only new clause in the covenant made to Noah, and all of the points in this covenant were without stated conditions. The sign of the covenant was the rainbow, which Noah could observe but could not enter into as a participant.

Covenants or Promises?

God's basic revelation to Noah was that He was a speaking God who saves. It is not until Abraham that we have a full unveiling of God as a covenant-making and covenant-keeping God. It was the spoken Word of God, not the covenants of God, that motivated Noah.

58

Noah related to God and functioned in life throughout the construction of the ark and the subsequent flood by leaning on God's promises and following God's instructions; the covenant God made with him came after the ark rested securely on Mount Ararat. It was the spoken Word of God, not the covenants of God, that motivated Noah.

It does not take an operation of the gift of discernment to recognize that far more Christians appropriate God by His promises than ever enter into covenants with Him. They tend to go in and out of the promises of God according to their needs rather than to live in a permanent relationship with God. They plead the promises when under pressure, but they keep the conditions only long enough to get the promised result. In the time of Moses, the mixed multitude walked in God's promises, but they never came into the covenants of God. We have no evidence that any of them ever entered the promised land. Perhaps they all perished in the wilderness, for no inheritance was ever provided for them except through marriage to the covenant people of God.

Our American churches are full of this mixed multitude who come to the God of promise but never cut covenant with Him. They happily eat His manna, drink His water and enjoy His divine protection, but they will not pay the price to enter into His covenant. What they fail to realize is that while God has no binding commitment from them, neither do they have a binding commitment from Him. They consistently negotiate with God in time of need and basically ignore Him in time of plenty. They constantly fight the same battles and live in the same insecurities because they are still only engaged to God, having never entered into a marriage union with Him.

Far too many Christians don't know the difference between standing on the promises and living in the covenants. When they are despondent, they cannot look at the stars above them and the sand beneath their feet and know that heaven and earth are pledged to fulfill God's will in their lives. Sickness sends them into panic, for they have no covenant with *Jehovah-Rapha* ("the Lord that healeth thee"). Financial reverses cause deep fear, since they have not cut covenant with *Jehovah-Jireh* ("the Lord will provide"). They forever lean upon God's mercy to meet His promises instead of coming into a relationship where they merely depend upon God's faithfulness to honor His covenants.

Like thousands of immigrants to America who have not become U.S. citizens, many of the persons in our churches are "green card" Christians. They have an official right to be among God's people, but they have no rights of citizenship, and they must regularly reregister to maintain their "green card" status. If they desire only survival and a higher standard of life, the green card will suffice, but if they want security of life and participation in the decisions that affect that life, they need to come into a covenantal relationship of naturalization. It is God's pleasure to bring us into the "family of God" through the sanctifying work of the Holy Spirit. This brings us beyond the promises into the covenants of God.

God's Covenant to Abraham

The great Abrahamic covenant is recorded in Genesis 15, and it begins with the Hebrew words *Debar Jehovah*, "the word of the Lord came to Abram" (v. 1). This is the first occurrence of this remarkable phrase that later became so common in the Hebrew Scriptures. The term naturally suggests the idea of audible and articulate sounds by which the Lord made known His will to mankind. While God did not always employ a vocal address, He did so on several occasions—when He addressed Moses in the tabernacle (see Num. 7:89), when He addressed Nebuchadnezzar (see Dan. 4:31) and when he addressed Paul (see Acts 9:4).

Scholars are quick to point out that the phraseology of this verse does not demand an audible voice. It may well have been but a direct influence upon Abraham's mind, originating a train of ideas far beyond the ordinary range of human thoughts. If so, these impressions came with such unusual vividness and force that they convinced Abraham of their supernatural source.

Whether audible or conceptual, this *Debar Jehovah* came "in a vision" (Gen. 15:1). In the Scriptures a vision is distinct from a dream in that the recipient of a divine vision was fully awake. His mind, supernaturally elevated, was entirely absorbed in the contemplation of objects apart from the influence of material impressions. Generally a vision concerned things unconnected with any former experience of the recipient. Yet the supernatural scene was, by the intense excitement of his faculties, as distinctly real to his mental vision as if he had gained the knowledge through the use of his bodily senses of sight, sound, touch or taste.

While the Bible distinguishes a vision from a dream, a vision could actually be imparted in a dream. In either case the Spirit of God moves upon the person's mind in such a way as to override any natural stimulation. Abraham seemed to have both a natural vision and a dream vision in this chapter.

Note that the expression "in a vision" applies to the whole fifteenth chapter. There is no pause anywhere, nor is there any sign that the vision ceased. There is absolutely no indication that the action was transferred to the sphere of the senses and of external reality. There is no textual reason to assume that somewhere there was a transition from the purely inward and spiritual sphere to the outward sphere of the senses. Everything that God said, did, displayed or caused Abraham to do was part of this very real vision. Actually, the entire revelation ended in a prophetic sleep, which also bears the character of a vision.

This covenant with Abraham came in vision form, but a vision wrought by God is not a mere fancy or a subjective play of thoughts. It is a spiritual fact which in all respects is as real as things discernible by the senses. Because we are so earthbound and sense-oriented, we are usually blind and deaf to the spiritual world. But the spiritual world can be made as real as our natural world by action of God, for we know that "the things which are seen were not made of things which are visible" (Heb. 11:3). Such visions produce a lasting significance superior to natural, physical acts and events for in them we touch timeless eternity. In this chapter we see time capsulized as Abraham moved from day to night in a single vision, going from the natural world into the spiritual realm of God's presence, where God talked with him and interacted with him.

Fellowship Endows Covenants

As it was with Abraham, it will be with us, for covenants with God are made in times of deep spiritual fellowship. God's covenant with Abraham was not merely an agreement regarding certain mutual rights and obligations—that could have been accomplished by a sacrificial transaction wherein God and Abraham would have discussed these rights, just as God and Noah had discussed the building and loading of the ark. God's covenant with Abraham was designed to establish the purely spiritual relation of a living fellowship between God and His man. It had such a deep inward meaning that nothing but a spiritual intuition and experience could give Abraham a firm grasp and permanent hold upon it. Things that are merely naturally discerned seldom create deep spiritual commitment.

Perhaps one reason so few Christians seem to walk in covenant relationship with God is that they have not entered into a deep spiritual relationship with Him. We live in a shallow generation both naturally and spiritually. Few genuinely seek the face of God in prayer and Bible reading. High spiritual experiences are time consuming, and we are unduly time conscious. One wonders how many modern Christians would actually give God an entire day to bring them into a lifetime covenant relationship. We want things done instantly, but a deep relationship takes time to develop, especially if it is a relationship between a person and God.

One of the great benefits of a covenant relationship with God—a deep personal relationship—is that the covenant can be made very clear. Questions can be asked when we are in the divine presence. Abraham didn't hesitate to ask God questions (see Gen. 15:2,8), and God satisfactorily answered them all. Furthermore, God reaffirmed all of His former promises to Abraham (see Gen. 15:7) and gave him the sign of the stars above (see Gen. 15:5). When the terms of the covenant were clear, God "cut" covenant with Abraham in the sacrifice of animals and birds (see Gen. 15:9,10,17). The words and the vision were sealed with the ceremonial offering of sacrifices to God, and God told Abraham about the future outworkings of the covenant (see Gen. 15:13-16). And so it is with us. God's covenants are not mere spiritual "feelings"; they are divine facts backed up by God's nature.

This Covenant Was Sealed

As was the custom of that day, God and Abraham sealed their covenant with a holocaust sacrifice. A three-year-old heifer, a three-year-old goat, a three-year-old ram, a turtledove and a pigeon were offered unto God as a certification of the covenant. Each of these animals was later described to Moses as a clean animal that could be offered to God as sacrifices. The requirement of "three-year-old animals" was probably based on the idea that three-year-old animals were in their prime, for God demands the very best of us.

In offering these oblations, Abraham split them in half and separated the carcasses, signifying that half of the sacrifice was for God and half was for Abraham. Both parties to the agreement identified with this blood sacrifice. Only the two birds were left unsegmented, as the Law later prescribed. Probably one was placed on either side.

When the vultures came to strip the carcasses clean, Abraham drove them off. Some see this as a foreshadowing of the Egyptians, who would treat Abraham's progeny as a vulture treats a carrion. Even the darkness and horror that Abraham experienced in this vision were most likely a foretaste of the slavery the Israelites would later experience, for in the midst of the terror, God said to Abraham, "Know certainly that your descendants will be strangers in a land that is not theirs, and they will afflict them four hundred years'' (Gen. 15:13). But in light of Christ's teaching that demons come like birds to snatch any spiritual seed or commitment from our lives, it may also refer to satanic opposition to our cutting covenant with God. Most of us have walked with God long enough to have learned that Satan surrenders territory very reluctantly, and that fear, horror and darkness are the primary tools of his trade.

Abraham sealed his covenant with God by sacrifice. We seal our covenant by faith expressed in a variety of ways. Some individuals are very sacramentally oriented; others find some type of ceremony to be useful to them. Some may seal their covenant with a season of prayer or a public affirmation of their faith. It seems, from Abraham's experience, that we need to make definite and concrete testimony to the spirit world and as a milestone to which we can return when our faith is being sorely tried. Whatever form of covenant sealing we may choose, God is willing to meet us; God is seeking our faith rather than the action that our faith may prompt.

The Protection of This Covenant

''And it came to pass, when the sun went down and it was dark, that behold, there was a smoking oven and a burning torch that passed between those pieces'' (Gen. 15:17). It is indisputable that this fire was God who demonstrated Himself in this manner on several occasions—in the bush that burned in front of Moses and in the pillar of fire that led Israel through the Sinai desert. The New Testament quotes the Old Testament in declaring, ''Our God is a consuming fire'' (Heb. 12:29), and the Acts of the Apostles says that the new covenant God made with His church was sealed with tongues of fire (see Acts 2:3).

This smoking oven and burning torch that Abraham saw were the Lord Himself passing between the pieces of the sacrifices as an external evidence that He condescended to enter into covenant with Abraham. We do not know that this burning fire consumed the sacrifices, but it is certainly implied, and God subsequently would instigate sacrifices that were to be wholly consumed with the divine fire.

"Cutting covenant" with God will always bring us into contact with the fire of God. In his testimony concerning Jesus, John the Baptist said, "I indeed baptize you with water unto repentance, but He who is coming after me is mightier than I, whose sandals I am not worthy to carry. He will baptize you with the Holy Spirit and fire" (Matt. 3:11). It appears to me that during the past decade thousands of persons have "received the baptism" without the fire. Content with a momentary "speaking with tongues," they fail to remain in God's presence to be sealed with God's fire, many who "speak with tongues" live lives totally unaffected by the covenant they looked at but did not enter. They do not "live in the Spirit" or "walk in the Spirit," nor are they "led by the Spirit," as Paul enjoined the saints (see Gal. 5:16,18,25). They seem to be content to "speak by the Spirit" without allowing God's Holy Spirit to burn away the dross, carnality and outright sinfulness in their lives. There is no covenant relationship present that brings the fire.

One of the purposes of God's entering into this covenant with Abraham was to reveal Himself as "a consuming fire." While the passage in Hebrews, "Our

God is a consuming fire,'' ends with a period, the Deuteronomy account from which it is quoted has a comma and is followed by another phrase: "The Lord your God is a consuming fire, a jealous God'' (4:24). This would seem to place this fire in the realm of the emotions—as an expression of jealousy.

God Is a Jealous God

The Hebrew word for "jealous" is *gana*, and this root occurs at least 878 times in the Old Testament. The word expresses a very strong emotion; some quality or possession of the object is desired by the subject. In a favorable sense it denotes consuming zeal focused on one that is loved, as David used it in saying, "Zeal for Your house has eaten me up'' (Ps. 69:9). However, when it is used in a derogatory sense, it indicates hostile and disruptive passions, as suggested in the saying "Wrath is cruel and anger a torrent, but who is able to stand before jealousy?'' (Prov. 27:4).

When *gana* is used for one's own property, it is translated "jealousy," but when it is used for another's property, it is rendered "envy.'' In the first case *gana* would speak of an impulse to protect, while in the latter circumstance it would indicate an inordinate eagerness to possess.

In the Deuteronomy passage, the noun form—*ganna*—is used. This form appears only in the Pentateuch, where it is used five times, exclusively of God. Each of the five occurrences is found in a context of idolatry and seems to depict the jealousy that God has for His earthly bride. As a husband holds his wife to himself and resists anything or anyone that would replace him in her affections, so God relates to His people. The prophets declared this in saying, "I am zealous for Jerusalem and for Zion with great zeal" (Zech. 1:14) and "God is jealous, and the Lord avenges" (Nah. 1:2).

To come into a covenant love relationship with God is to expose ourselves to God's great jealousy. His zeal for us causes Him to oppose anything and everything that would attempt to break our union with Him. Once we cut covenant, we are God's and His alone. Embracing another love is adulterous idolatry that brings us face to face with God's jealousy. This may seem cruel and harsh if we have turned our hearts to other lovers, as Israel repeatedly did during the time of the prophets, but it is actually merciful that God will not allow us to abandon a cut covenant. God has not made provision for divorce from His covenant people.

God's jealousy can be comforting, for God's protective anger continuously accompanies us. Anything and everything that would replace Him in our affections must deal with His wrath. He is our protector and defense. His jealousy for us becomes wrath toward the enemy. Satan knows that when he entices or touches one who is in a covenant relationship with God, he must deal with God Himself—a formidable foe.

God Is a Consuming Fire

It is not just that God is a fire; He is a *consuming* fire, as both the Old and New Testaments declare: "The Lord your God is a consuming fire." God is consuming not in the sense that He is sustained by that which He consumes, as is the case with most fire, but in the connotation that everything He touches is consumed by Him. Just as the gas starter flame in the fireplace will start a fire in a log and transform the static energy of the log into a similar flame, so God feeds upon Himself, but in sharing Himself with us He becomes a consuming fire.

Fire transforms energy from one form to another—from solids, such as coal and wood, to heat, light, moisture and smoke. Similarly, God transforms our nature into His nature with His consuming fire of love and jealousy. We who were carnal become spiritual when we are in His fire. When the fire of God's love is burning within us, we are being transformed by the presence of almighty God into the very image of God. He consumes our minds, emotions and will causing them to come into the divine image through the process of God's consuming fire.

The greatest difference among Christians is not their education, consecration or experience; it is how much of God's fire they have allowed to burn in their lives. Some persons get close enough to God to get warm. Others stand close enough to produce smoke. A few allow God to consume them wholly with His presence. This has been the testimony of saints in the Bible. To Jeremiah, God said, "Behold, I will make My words in your mouth fire, and this people wood, and it shall devour them" (Jer. 5:14). Much later, Jeremiah testified, "From above He has sent fire into my bones, and it overpowered them" (Lam. 1:13). The two disciples on the Emmaus road testified, "Did not our heart burn within us while He talked with us on the road, and while He opened the Scriptures to us?" (Luke 24:32). Isaiah was purged with a burning coal from heaven's golden altar and became God's messenger (see Is. 6:6,9). God's fire was transforming in them, and it will be so in us.

Worship Requires a Covenantal Relationship

True worship requires a covenant to bring us into the necessary intimacy with God. The uncommitted may have an awe of God, and even strong religious feelings about God, but since worship is two lovers responding to each other, we must enter into a covenant relationship with God to enter into true worship, for covenants offer both authority and availability. Much like the covenant of marriage, God offers to "cut covenant" with us and bring us into a protective shelter where worship can be released with full assurance of its acceptance.

When we enter into worship without first entering into a covenant with God, we may find ourselves worshipping something short of God. If God is not the object of our worship, we are involved in idol worship; no matter where it takes place or how we are performing it, for when anything or anyone other than God becomes the object of our worship, it is an idol to us. Worship of pleasant religious sensations is self-worship. Worship of doctrine, creed, theology or experience is tradition-worship—the very thing Christ condemned so severely. Worship of a pastor or leader is hero-worship no different from that of sports figures or singing stars. Even the veneration of power, position or prestige is idolatry ipso facto. Forms of idolatry can become very real to those who engage in them, but that doesn't make them acceptable to the living God.

Jesus said of the Samaritans, "You worship what you do not know; we know what we worship" (John 4:22). It is possible to have some of the elements of worship—perhaps admiration, self-abasement, surrender, attachment—and not be among the redeemed at all. Only God is worthy of our worship, and He is a jealous God who has offered to enter into a covenantal relationship with us whereby He becomes the exclusive object of our worship, and we, in turn, become the objects of His protective and providential love.

The Hebrews passage that describes God as "a consuming fire" states, "Therefore, since we are receiving a kingdom which cannot be shaken, let us have grace, by which we may serve God acceptably with reverence and godly fear. For our God is a consuming fire" (12:28,29). The subject is worship, and the reason given for entering into worship is "for our God is a consuming fire." Our God is worthy of being served "acceptably with reverence and godly fear." Actually, the worship of our loving God is mankind's whole reason for existence. It is why God redeemed us, and it is why He formed a church here on the earth. The Christian church exists to worship God first, last and always.

God deeply desires to be worshipped, but we must learn that we cannot have our own way and worship God just as we please. We have entered into His covenant, and everything must be done His way—but remember, "The law of the Lord is perfect, converting the soul" (Ps. 19:7). The God who desires our fellowship is not hard to please, although He may prove to be hard to satisfy. He expects of us only what He Himself has supplied in the covenant that He has offered. He is quick to mark every simple effort to please Him, and He is just as quick to overlook our imperfections when He knows that we meant to do His will, for He is not only a God of the covenant; He is a moral God—a God of love—as Moses happily discovered.

chapter four

MOSES MET A
MORAL GOD

"...a God of truth and without injustice...."
(Deuteronomy 32:4)

From the moment that Moses was placed in the small boat constructed from the rushes that grew along the banks of the river Nile, he was experiencing a covenant-keeping God. By the edict of Pharaoh, the baby Moses should have been drowned, but his parents maintained a faith in the promises made to Abraham and they refused to succumb to the king's commands. The events that followed—from Moses' being drawn out of the water by Pharaoh's daughter to Miriam's cleverness in securing Moses' own mother as his nurse—prove that this was a divine intervention.

Quite obviously the concept of a speaking and a covenant-making God had stayed with mankind. Abraham passed it on to Isaac and Isaac taught it to his son, for Jacob met God at Bethel, heard God's voice and entered into covenant with Jehovah.

In the days of Jacob and Joseph, God tested the fidelity

of His people by bringing them to Egypt. Slowly their relationship with the Egyptians deteriorated from being a favored people to being flogged slaves. Although Joseph demonstrated an amazing ability to hear from God, from the time of his death until the incident of the burning bush we have no indication of a word from God or of any further revelation of God. For four hundred years the Israelites consistently accommodated their worsening circumstances and adjusted to having no manifestation of God among them. Unfortunately, throughout history people often have adapted to an absence of God rather than persevered into His presence. Any covenant into which God has entered with mankind is perpetual and can be exercised by meeting the stated conditions. Rather than to seek and meet these conditions, most of us prefer to look at the sovereignty of God and lay the blame on Him. How His heart must ache when He is blamed for the absence of the relationship He has so earnestly sought to re-establish with people.

Moses Met God

Once again God took the initiative to inaugurate contact with His chosen people. More than any man before him, Moses seemed to be destined for a confrontation with God. Although he was miraculously spared from destruction and was meticulously trained in the arts and sciences of Egypt, he did not meet God in Egypt's university nor did his political power there bring him into a relationship with God. Only after forty years on the Sinai desert shepherding sheep did Moses begin to know God intimately.

When he was given his commission at the burning bush, Moses met a speaking God who spoke as specifically to him as He had to Noah. It was the beginning of forty years of communication with God such as no one before or since has experienced. Moses was privileged to speak to God through the angel in the burning bush, but at the giving of the Law on Mount Sinai, Moses spoke to God face to face.

In the river Nile, Moses met a covenant God and later he realized that his commission was to enable God to fulfill the covenant He had made with Abraham by bringing his progeny out of Egyptian bondage into the land that God had promised to Abraham and his seed. Few if any men have so cherished God's covenants and have held Jehovah accountable for fulfilling them.

While Moses entered into the prior revelations of God, he was the first person after Adam who came to know a moral God. The revelation of Himself that God gave to Moses on the mountain was a violation of everything he had been taught in Egypt. The gods of the Egyptians had been visualized as animals with supernatural powers. Actually, each of the ten plagues that God poured out in Egypt was against one of their many deities. Moses had been taught that bestiality and divinity were one and the same. Furthermore, the gods of the nations around Horeb or Sinai, where Moses spent forty years tending sheep, were cruel, harsh, exacting deities who seemed to be unfeeling and without compassion toward mankind.

In the midst of this background, Moses caught a glimpse of a God who was not only just but who was the justifier of those who sought Him. He met a God of moral perfection, a God who would forgive and forget. He was confronted by a God who deeply loved mankind and who was committed to their good. What a contrast this was to Egyptian theology, and what an enlargement upon revealed theology. Noah had met a God of judgment who showed grace to a favored son; Abraham had met a God who entered into a covenant with a favored family; but Moses met a moral God who spared and covenanted with an entire nation—not because they desired or deserved it, but because God had purposed it.

Moses Met a God Who
Was Moral in His Commitments

More than half a century before Moses' birth, God had promised Abraham, "I will bless those who bless you, and I will curse him who curses you..." (Gen. 12:3). Moses watched God ruin Egypt to keep this pledge. As Moses raised his rod again and again to bring plague after plague upon the people who had so cursed the children of Israel with the bondage of slavery, he must have anticipated the saying that is now a cliche to us: "Although the wheels of God grind slowly, they grind exceedingly fine."

Even though it was unlikely that anyone on earth had a clear understanding of God's covenant with Abraham, God felt bound by His own nature to perform everything He had promised. God does not honor His covenants because people keep pressing their claims; God honors His word because of His unvarying nature. Moses discovered that God is truth and that He is not changed by the passing of time or by the forgetfulness of mankind.

Everything God did during the forty-plus years it took to get Israel out of Egypt and into the promised land was done because of the moral commitments he had made to Abraham. Although Israel murmured and rebelled in the wilderness on ten or more occasions, God merely chastened them—He never abandoned them. Not until the first generation refused to enter Canaan because of the evil report of ten of the twelve elders who spied out the land did God purpose to destroy them and begin a new race of people through Moses.

Moses was not interested in becoming the father of a new race of people; he was committed to bringing Israel into the land that "flowed with milk and honey." Prostrate before God, Moses began to intercede with Jehovah, pleading God's moral nature (see Num. 14:11-19). "Because of who You are, You cannot do what You have threatened to do" was Moses' argument. Once again God's moral nature won out over His righteous anger, and He spared His people, although He chastened them severely. Moses learned that a commitment from God was eternal because of God's unchangeable moral nature. What reassurance this gave to Moses, and what comfort it has afforded the saints of all generations. If God said it, that settles it; He'll see to it!

Moses Met a God Who Was Moral in His Commandments

After the march out of Egypt and the deliverance at the Red Sea, God brought His people to Sinai, where, in the full hearing of all Israel, He spoke the terms of His covenant with the nation. They had already seen great demonstrations of God's power both in Egypt and in the wilderness, and they were participants in God's great mercy and grace as evidenced in His protection and provision, but now they were being introduced to the Ten Commandments that God called His covenant (see Deut. 4:13). Four of these covenantal terms dealt with Israel's relationship with God, while six of the commandments dealt with their horizontal relationships with one another. No greater summary of morality has ever been written.

After the public declaration of this covenant, God called Moses to the top of Mount Sinai, where God greatly enlarged His covenant. For forty days God communicated to Moses the Law, the commandments, the judgments and the statutes (see Deut. 4:44,45). These, too, covered their relationship with God and with each other. They formed a moral code that enabled a vast congregation of people to live together harmoniously. These statutes dealt with a criminal code, sanitation, food handling, sexual relationships, property ownership, laws of inheritance and ownership of chattel property. This has formed the philosophy of and basis for all English law.

The Law as given to Moses dealt with everything from an introduction of God and His nature to ways of approaching Him. A large section of the commandments concerned the construction of a tabernacle that would bring God's presence into the camp of Israel and become a means whereby unholy people could approach a holy God. Laws and regulations regarding the priesthood, the sacrifices, the rituals and all the ceremonies provided a means of approach that was acceptable to God. People were not left to the caprice of God; they were brought into the covenants of God.

These very laws were moral laws that declared God as One who worked according to predetermined principles, and He was willing to share the natural and spiritual laws with His people. Whether they were growing a tree or establishing a priesthood, God defined the principles that would make their efforts successful. They did not have to understand the principle completely to make it work; they merely had to apply it as directed.

Moses' three trips up the mountain to converse with God convinced him that God works according to divine principles and governs according to divine laws. As the psalmist would later say, "Your way, O God, is in the sanctuary" (Ps. 77:13). When will we learn that God's laws and principles are dependent not upon our comprehension but upon our cooperation? A child need not know anything about the laws of reproduction to plant a bean and reap a harvest. He does what he is told to do, and the laws of reproduction do the rest. We need not become as wise as God to enjoy Him; we need only to cooperate with His laws to enjoy His presence and His benefits.

Moses Met a God Who Was Moral in His Character

After God finished giving the Law the second time, Moses requested to see Him. In response to this request, God hid Moses in a cleft of a rock and covered him with His hand. He passed by and allowed Moses to see His afterglow; but this did not satisfy Moses, so God passed by a second time, and that time He proclaimed the divine name.

At the burning bush, Moses had learned God's secret name: Jehovah, or YHWH. This was translated as the "I AM"—the "self-existent One"—and it revealed God as eternal, uncaused, unconditioned, self-sufficient and all-powerful. This proved to be sufficient revelation to bring Israel out of Egypt, but YHWH had not revealed God's nature to Moses.

Now that the Law had been given and the people were entering into a covenant relationship with God, it was necessary for Moses and the people to know something of the nature of the God to whom they were pledging allegiance. The revelation of YHWH and His subsequent action implies moral attributes, but this enlarged revelation of God's name declares moral attributes.

God's verbal revelation of Himself was recorded by Moses: "Then the Lord descended in the cloud and stood with him there, and proclaimed the name of the Lord. And the Lord passed before him and proclaimed, 'The Lord, the Lord God, merciful and gracious, long-suffering and abounding in goodness and truth, keeping mercy for thousands, forgiving iniquity and transgression and sin, by no means clearing the guilty...' " (Ex. 34:5-7).

This is the first full revelation of God's nature, and it is given as the name of God. There is no verb in the proclamation, for all of this is the name of God. It is not that the Lord extends mercy and grace; it is "the Lord, merciful and gracious." Each term is part of the name and nature of God. This is what He is, not what He does. At the burning bush, God told Moses what He as Jehovah would do—deliver His people from bondage. Now He declared what He—as Jehovah—is. First the revelation was in deeds; now it is in words. At the bush, the emphasis was upon the name, but at Sinai the emphasis was on the character of Him who bears the name.

The Lord God

The first descriptive words that God spoke to Moses about Himself (at the burning bush) were "Jehovah, Jehovah El," or "the Self-existent, the Self-existent God." What had been revealed before is now confirmed, for fresh revelation is never contradictory to previous revelation.

We must believe in the person of God before we can believe in His character. Until we know Him as God we cannot know Him as a God of love. "He who comes to God must believe that He is, and that He is a rewarder of those who diligently seek Him" (Heb. 11:6). First we meet Him; then we come to know Him. Long after his Damascus road experience, Paul cried, "That I may know Him and the power of His resurrection, and the fellowship of His sufferings, being conformed to His death" (Phil. 3:10). All attempts to know God without first having an introductory confrontation with Him are doomed to failure from the start, for God cannot be known through search and study; He must reveal Himself to us.

Moses met God at the burning bush and became an instrument through whom God worked mighty signs and wonders, but there was a deep and lasting longing in Moses to know this God. In response to Moses' request to see God, Jehovah spoke six positive statements about Himself, using terms that are almost synonymous. It is a threefold description of the triune God's essential nature: mercy, truth, justice. All future revelations of His nature would fit in these three categories.

Jehovah...Merciful

The first quality of His nature that God declared was His mercy. "Jehovah...merciful" was His cry. The Hebrew word used here for mercy is *rakhum* (or *rachum*)—"the tender or pitiful one." In his book *Synonyms of the Old Testament*, Robert Girdlestone says, "Mercy is really the same thing as pity, though the words have gradually assumed rather different senses." The prophets used this word *rachum* to express the tenderness with which God regards His downcast people, and it is often translated "compassion" and "bowels of compassion" in the King James Version.

How incredibly precious that mercy is mentioned first, for this is the fountain from which all the other characteristics of God's nature flow. It was God's mercy that was David's hope when he sinned so grievously. He pled with the prophet Gad, "Please let us fall into the hand of the Lord, for His mercies are great" (2 Sam. 24:14). From experience David knew that, although God was capable of far greater destruction than any force on earth, Jehovah was merciful by nature and that these mercies could be entreated through repentance. Much later in Israel's history, God told Jeremiah to proclaim, "Return, back-sliding Israel," says the Lord, "and I will not cause My anger to fall on you; for I am merciful" (Jer. 3:12).

"Jehovah...merciful" was the message of the tabernacle, for the very throne on which God sat was called the mercy seat. Because God delights in mercy, not in judgment, His throne on earth is called the mercy seat, not the judgment throne. When God is among His people, His heart is touched with their misery, and they become the object of God's pity. David said, "As a father pities his children, so the Lord pities those who fear Him" (Ps. 103:13). All of the religious projections of God as a harsh, judgmental being run contrary to the self-revelation that God gave to us through Moses. God is first and foremost merciful.

Keeping Mercy for Thousands

Jehovah goes on to define Himself as merciful by using the phrase "keeping mercy for thousands." The Hebrew word is *notser-khesed*, meaning "the keeper of mercy.'' God does not desert those whom He loves, but He is merciful to them and their children. The usual renderings for this word in the King James Version are kindness, goodness, pity, favor, mercy and lovingkindness. As God said of David, ''My lovingkindness I will not utterly take from him, nor allow My faithfulness to fail'' (Ps. 89:33). The RSV and other translations use the term ''steadfast love,'' for *khesed* always has the overtone of loyalty to an agreement.

It is not merely that God keeps mercy, but He keeps mercy ''for thousands.'' All of the Jewish Targums render this as ''keeping mercy to a thousand generations.'' While the visitation of sin is viewed as extending only ''unto the third and fourth generation,'' mercy is kept for ''thousands'' or ''a thousand generations.'' How accurately the Word declares, ''But the mercy of the Lord is from everlasting to everlasting on those who fear Him, and His righteousness to children's children'' (Ps. 103:17). Paul later put it this way: ''Where sin abounded, grace abounded much more'' (Rom. 5:20).

God does good to those who trust in His mercy at present and reserves good for them in the future; and not for them only, but even for their children and grandchildren. Little wonder, then, that Psalm 136 says twenty-six times, ''For His mercy endures forever.''

Jehovah...Gracious

Perhaps because the Law declared that ''by the mouth of two or three witnesses the matter shall be established'' (Deut. 19:15) or maybe because God is a triune God or possibly for the sake of emphasis by repetition, when speaking to Moses God refers to Himself a third time as being a God of mercy: ''Jehovah...gracious.'' Here the writer used the Hebrew word *khannun*, which would

83

be more properly translated "the gracious One" or "He who bestows His benefits out of mere favor, without obligation." This adjective form of the word is used only of God and pictures the action which springs from His free and unmerited love and tender affection to His people.

Unless God's goodness was free, spontaneous and unconstrained, man could never enjoy it, for he cannot purchase it, earn it or deserve it—he can only receive it. As Paul stated, "For you know the grace of our Lord Jesus Christ, that though He was rich, yet for your sakes He became poor, that you through His poverty might become rich" (2 Cor. 8:9). Jehovah is not only merciful—He is "merciful and gracious." David, Hezekiah, Isaiah, Joel, Malachi and others recognized that God's graciousness is the grounds on which God bestows His mercies. In a time of distress, David cried, "But You, O Lord, are a God full of compassion, and gracious, longsuffering and abundant in mercy" (Ps. 86:15).

As if to reinforce all He had told Moses about His merciful nature, Jehovah added, "abundant in goodness." The Hebrew word is *rab-khesed*, which means "the great in mercy." It is translatable as "the bountiful being; He who is exuberant in His beneficence."

Mercy is more than abundant; mercy rules in the character of God. There is no limit to God's goodness. It is a perpetual fountain that is never exhausted, for it flows from His very nature, and "He cannot deny Himself" (2 Tim. 2:13). To know Him is to know mercy, for one is inseparable from the other. Merciful, gracious and abundant in goodness are God's names. "Sing to the Lord, bless His name" (Ps. 96:2).

Jehovah...Abounding in Truth

Having identified Himself as merciful, Jehovah next defined His nature as truth. The Hebrew word is *emeth*—"the truth or true One." It signifies steadfastness, as implied in the word "amen." It is translated "verity" in Psalm 111:7: "The works of His hands are verity and justice."

David sang to Jehovah, "Your truth reaches to the clouds" (Ps. 108:4) and "the truth of the Lord endures forever" (Ps. 117:2). This truth springs from the immutability of God. From Jehovah, the fountain of truth, flow all wisdom and knowledge. Men cannot discover truth by hard thinking; it is always revealed by the Spirit. Jesus emphasized this in saying, "However, when He, the Spirit of truth, has come, He will guide you into all truth" (John 16:13).

Man's knowledge of truth is not theoretical but comes through a vital encounter with Christ, for, taken to its prime, truth is Jesus. Didn't He say, "I am the way, the truth, and the life" (John 14:6)? In this sense, then, truth is more than a right correlation of facts; truth is a person—Jesus.

There can be no trust in any being who is not true; truth is therefore a prerequisite to worship, for God is the only acceptable object of worship, and He is absolute verity and truth. We can trust Him in every revelation He has made of Himself and in everything that He has promised or threatened, for by His very nature "it is impossible for God to lie" (Heb. 6:18). This becomes the very foundation of our worship, since His constancy and veracity enable us to move into His presence with full assurance of faith and an absolute conviction of acceptance.

Just as surely as God's truth is fundamental to our worship, so Christ told the Samaritan woman that our truth is imperative to worship: "God is Spirit, and those who worship Him must worship in spirit and truth" (John 4:24). Neither "spirit" nor "truth" is capitalized, for they refer not to Jesus but to our spirit and to the truth that is within us. Nothing will prevent our worship more than deceit, no matter how religious it may be. Even sin is less a preventive to worship than is deceit. God—*the* truth—must be worshipped in truth!

Jehovah...Justice

Jehovah is the God of both mercy and justice. He introduces His justice by the Hebrew phrase *nakkeh lo yenakkeh*, which means "the righteous judge" but which we have translated as "long-suffering." The thrust of the Hebrew speaks of One who distributes justice with an impartial hand, with whom no innocent person can ever be condemned. This is Jehovah!

God's justice is an essential part of His nature, and it is a necessary consequence of His love. God is both just and the justifier of mankind, as Paul told the church at Rome: "To demonstrate at the present time His righteousness, that He might be just and the justifier of the one who has faith in Jesus" (Rom. 3:26).

God is long-suffering. He is good not by spasm or effort but by His own eternal being. He is patient and unwearied; He is "slow to anger" and "bears long." Even when the wrongs of His saints call for vengeance, God is long-suffering! Hallelujah! And because He is long-suffering with us, He distributes justice with an impartial hand. He does not lash out at us to relieve His frustrations, as we sometimes do to our children. If He chastens us, it is in love and is done for our own good.

If He judges us, it is always consistent with His law and balanced with His mercy. He is indeed the judge who "shall judge the peoples righteously" (Ps. 96:10).

Jehovah...Forgiving

Almost contrary to our normal concepts of a righteous judge, God defines Himself as "forgiving iniquity and transgression and sin." The Hebrew is *nos 'avon vapesha vekhattaah*, which means "the forgiver of iniquity and transgression and sin." The original language is consistent with the definition of God, while our English version tends to lower it to an action of God—"forgiving." God is the being who alone can forgive sin and give peace to the guilty soul. Men may try to deal with guilt, but only God is the "forgiver."

This Hebrew word for forgive signifies a lifting up and taking away. God had already demonstrated this in the provision of the scapegoat whereby Israel's sins would be imputed to a goat that would be released in an uninhabited place as a symbol of the people's sins being laid on another and carried out of sight. The prophet Isaiah may well have alluded to this when he wrote, "All we like sheep have gone astray; we have turned, every one, to his own way; and the Lord has laid on Him the iniquity of us all" (Is. 53:6). What he said is that Jehovah imputed our sins to Jesus, who lifted them up at Calvary and carried them away. Confessed sins and iniquities are removed, never again to be remembered against us. "Therefore if the Son makes you free, you shall be free indeed," Jesus said in John 8:36. God is the great forgiver because He, through Jesus, became our sin-bearer.

The great theologian Paul expressed it this way: "For all have sinned and fall short of the glory of God, being justified freely by His grace through the redemption that is in Christ Jesus, whom God set forth to be a propitiation by His blood, through faith, to demonstrate His righteousness, because in His forbearance God had passed over the sins that were previously committed, to demonstrate at the present time His righteousness, that He might be just and the justifier of the one who has faith in Jesus'' (Rom. 3:23-26).

God declared that He, the forgiver, was forgiving iniquity and transgression and sin. In so saying, He was not expressing meaningless repetitions of the same idea but was dealing with separate concepts, for these terms describe different phases and shades of evil.

Iniquity is literally a ''twisting'' or ''something twisted.'' It speaks of a violation. Iniquitous sin is deviation from a standard to which we ought to be conformed. Iniquity twists God's law to man's desires and ends up twisting the man to deformity. Jewish writers say that iniquity signifies sins through pride and presumption, and they may be right in their view, for these are common causes for twisting God's Word.

Transgression is literally the ''shaking off of obedience to God.'' While iniquity deals with abstract thought of law, transgression deals with the lawgiver. The very center of sin is the shaking off of obedience to God. It is graphically illustrated in the garden of Eden when Adam shook off obedience to God to eat of the forbidden fruit. His sin has become the common sin of mankind; every person wants to go his or her own way, which is impossible without rejecting God's way. The Jewish writers classify transgression as ''rebellion against God.'' Perhaps we would be less insistent upon having our own way if we would see it as rebellion against God.

Sin, or at least the Hebrew word used here for sin, means "missing the mark." It comes from the imagery of the archer who stretches his bow and shoots short of the target. Every sin misses the goal at which we should be aiming. All sin is a failure. God made mankind in His own image, but look at what sin did to the race. Even though we set out to live good lives, we fail because of sin. The most successful person in the eyes of the world has a deep inner sense of failure unless his or her sin problem has been settled at the cross. Fame, fortune, power, beauty, ability and position cannot make anyone feel genuinely successful. All sinners instinctively know that they are failures. The Jews interpret sin as that which is committed through error and mistake, and this is what "missing the mark" is all about.

How wonderful it is that God's mercy and justice include the full and free forgiveness of every kind and degree of sin! No sin confessed will be unforgiven, and no sin unconfessed will go unpunished. When grace is refused, justice demands the full penalty of the law.

God added one further description of Himself to Moses in saying "by no means clearing the guilty." God's justice reveals the other side of His nature in punishing as well as forgiving the sinner. This attribute is essential, for without it God would not be God.

Recently an acquaintance of mine stood before a judge for sentencing on a charge of deliberate income tax evasion. He had been tried by a jury and found guilty. Before handing down the sentence, the judge asked him whether or not, if he was returned to society, he would go to work and make provision to pay his back taxes.

When the man declared that he would not because he felt it violated his constitutional rights, the judge sentenced him to a lengthy prison term. Because the judge's grace was rejected, the full penalty of the law was meted out. So it must be with righteous judgment, and God is a righteous judge! Repentance brings mercy; rejection brings judgment. There is no middle ground.

The poet Edward Young wisely wrote, "A God of all mercy is a God unjust." The guilty may be spared so that they may repent, but they will not be cleared. They may prosper for a time, but a heavy retribution awaits them. God is merciful and good, but none is pardoned except those who repent and forsake the practice of sin. God is "the Lord merciful" but "by no means clearing the guilty."

Moses Worshipped the God He Met

The sacred record tells us, "So Moses made haste and bowed his head toward the earth, and worshiped" (Ex. 34:8). Moses had seen a moral God, and the only sensible action was to worship Him!

The very nature of God makes worshipping Him desirable. "God is love" (1 John 4:16), and who can resist love? God is merciful, and we desperately need mercy. God is long-suffering and abounding in goodness and truth, and this is like a permanent magnet drawing us as worshippers into His presence. Like the angels in heaven who cried, "Worthy is the Lamb who was slain" (Rev. 5:12), so our hearts also plead God's worth to be worshipped.

Furthermore, the laws by which God operates make it possible for us to approach Him, knowing in advance that we will be accepted. Jesus told His disciples, "All that the Father gives Me will come to Me, and the one who comes to Me I will by no means cast out" (John 6:37). The worshipper who approaches God by the prescribed route has full assurance of an audience with God. Such a worshipper comes by invitation and needs not fear rejection.

When a person meets a moral God, worship is a natural response, for our moral nature came from God, so that portion of us that yearns for God is "deep call[ing] unto deep" (Ps. 42:7). Actually, we can be satisfied only when our moral nature reaches into and touches the nature of a moral God. In this sense, then, worship originates with God and comes back to us and is reflected from us as in a mirror. This is worship totally acceptable to God.

Responding to God's moral nature moves the worshipper past the boundaries of gratitude. Most Christians express grateful responses to their God, but we all need to learn to respond to God in admiration and exaltation of His eternal excellence, for while praise speaks of God's mighty deeds, worship is concerned with His marvelous person. We must rise beyond thanking God for the benefits we have received from Him and worship Him for the being He has revealed Himself to be. Loving God's deeds may produce awe, but loving His nature [name] induces worship.

Concepts Control Worship

We will never worship God at levels higher than our concepts of God; lofty worship demands lofty concepts of God. David sang, "Let all those rejoice who put their trust in You; let them ever shout for joy, because You defend them; let those also who love Your name be joyful in You" (Ps. 5:11). We are to be joyful in the Lord, to express our worship of the Lord because we trust in

God and in the name of God.

How can anyone ever worship God acceptably without knowing what kind of God He really is? Cain couldn't. Cain surely did not know the true character of God. He did not believe that the matter of sin was eternally important to God, so he did things "his way," and his worship was not accepted by God. In contrast to Cain, the Samaritan woman at Jacob's well caught a glimpse of who Jesus really was, and when she did, she worshipped Him in spirit and in truth. And so will we, for our concepts control our responses.

These concepts form progressively. A new convert cannot have a mature concept of God. God's plan of self-revelation moves from the known into the unknown by progressive steps. The prophet Isaiah asked, "Whom will he teach knowledge? And whom will he make to understand the message? Those just weaned from milk? Those just drawn from the breasts? For precept must be upon precept, precept upon precept, line upon line, line upon line, here a little, there a little" (Is. 28:9,10). God begins by revealing His salvation, but He progresses until He is able to reveal the Savior! Initially we find Him as a need-meeter. Few, if any, come to God because they want Him, rather because they need Him. Albert Simpson, founder of the Christian and Missionary Alliance, once said, "I pass on to you this warning, that we may become so enamored with God's good gifts that we fail to worship the Giver."

The progression of revelation to Moses moved from seeing a God of vengeance in the plagues of Egypt to seeing a God of law to embracing a God of love. God's goal is that we should come to a knowledge of His true nature.

The wisest person in the world is the person who knows the most about God. Higher concepts of God produce higher levels of worship of God, but they also produce higher levels of personal satisfaction. A.W. Tozer wrote, "I believe that the reverential fear of God mixed with love and fascination and astonishment and admiration and devotion is the most enjoyable state and the most purifying emotion the human soul can know."

A true fear of God based upon a proper understanding of God is a beautiful thing, for it is worship, it is love, it is veneration. It is a high moral happiness because that is what God is.

No man between Adam and Moses had such a concept of a moral God, but many persons since Moses have met this same God of tenderness and have lived transformed lives because of it. God's goodness brought them to repentance (see Rom. 2:4), His graciousness brought them to salvation (see Eph. 2:8), and His forgiveness brought them into relationship with Himself.

Along with Moses, Joshua learned that God is a good God, but he also learned that divine goodness is not impotent—it is powerful. Following the death of Moses, Joshua participated in this mighty power of God and made that power available to those whom he led into the promised land.

chapter five

JOSHUA MET AN ALMIGHTY GOD

"I am God Almighty."
                        (Genesis 35:11)

The revelation that "God is good" is exhilarating and awe-inspiring, but it may lead us to passivity. The warmth and the comfort of being the objects of God's faithfulness can induce indolence and nonparticipation in God's covenants. If we become presumptuous in thinking that His mercy will excuse our disobedience, if we mistake His meekness for weakness or His pardon for permission, we may seek to manipulate God with worship rather than to relate to Him in wonder.

Paul reminded the Gentile church of this combination of affection and austerity in the nature of God when he wrote, "Therefore consider the goodness and severity of God: on those who fell, severity; but toward you, goodness, if you continue in His goodness. Otherwise you also will be cut off" (Rom. 11:22). Goodness *and* severity are both found in God.

God's goodness is an essential part of His nature. He

does not merely do good things; He is a good God, but sharing in this divine goodness is neither automatic nor unconditional. Participation in God's moral covenants requires obedience to the stated commandments. The promises of God based upon His moral law are "I will if you will."

In an interview on TV's "Today" show, Kurt Waldheim, then secretary general of the United Nations, commented that the most difficult part of his office was having nothing but moral power to back his position. It seems that right without might seldom leads to change. Just as a legislative body without executive reinforcement is little more than a committee with power to recommend, so a God who is only mercy is impotent to enforce His rules. We cannot have a proper concept of God unless we think of Him as all-powerful. He is God almighty. His Word contains no suggestions—only commandments, and He has the executive power to enforce those commandments.

Charles Spurgeon once said, "God's power is like Himself, self-existent, self-sustained. The mightiest of men cannot add so much as a shadow of increased power to the Omnipotent One. He sits on a buttressed throne and leans on no assisting arm. His court is not maintained by His courtiers, nor does it borrow its splendor from His creatures. He is Himself the great central source and Originator of all power."

While it is true that the Bible declares, "To the Lord our God belong mercy and forgiveness" (Dan. 9:9; see Ps. 62:12), the Scriptures equally declare that "power belongs to God" (Ps. 62:11). God did not acquire His power; it belongs to Him inherently. God and power are so inseparable that they are reciprocal. Jesus even used power as a name of God when He told the high priest, "You will see the Son of Man sitting at the right hand of the Power" (Mark 14:62), that is, at the right hand of God.

Often a mere demonstration of power is all the motivation people need to accept the provisions and requirements of moral law. A show of armed strength has often forced a world leader to accept moral or international law. The power to enforce often becomes the power to control. God is, indeed, a God of limitless grace, but He is equally a God of unlimited power. Fifty-seven times the Bible calls God "the Almighty," meaning that all power in the limitless span of creation and eternity finds its source in Him. God is the only being ever described as "almighty" throughout the Scriptures, for all other power and authority are delegated by Him, who alone is power and might.

Joshua, Moses' faithful servant and the second in command in Israel's camp, came to know this God of all might and power in a very intimate way. At first his knowledge was vicarious and was based upon observation, but later it was personal and vital.

Joshua Perceived God's Power

Joshua, or Hoshea as he was called in Egypt, was born about the time Moses fled from Egypt to the back side of the desert. By the time Moses returned to Egypt, Joshua was already a highly respected leader among his people, and there is every reason to believe that when Moses met with the elders, or leaders, of Israel before going in to confront Pharaoh, Joshua was present. What excitement he must have felt when Moses told them God was preparing to deliver Israel from bondage. How his eyes must have bulged when Moses' rod became a serpent, and when Moses picked it up by the tail it turned back into a shepherd's crook. Then Joshua watched Moses put his hand into the top of his toga and pull it out leprous, but on a repeat performance the hand was as whole as before. Joshua was experiencing his first view of the power of almighty God, but it certainly would not be his last. Forty years later he would be the channel through which God's power would be released among the Israelites. How mercifully God demonstrates His power *to* us before He releases His power *through* us.

What awe and wonder must have overwhelmed Joshua as he watched God's almightiness come against the chief Egyptian deities, from the sacred river Nile to the sacrosanct eldest sons of the Egyptians. The priests of Pharaoh were powerless to prevent this violation of the very gods they had led the Egyptians to worship, and even the most brilliant magicians were able to duplicate only the first two miracles God performed in their land.

Plague after plague fell on Egypt. The revolting blood for water, the annoying frogs, the embarrassing lice, the discomforting flies, the destructive diseases on the livestock, the painful boils on both man and beast, the damaging hail, the consuming locusts, the paralyzing darkness and finally the incredible slaughter of all the firstborn—these plagues built the Egyptians' depression to a crescendo that completely demoralized them. The fact that the land of Goshen, where the Hebrews lived, was exempted from all but the first three plagues merely confused the Egyptians further and offered God's people even more proof that all of this was the hand of God extended on their behalf.

Joshua watched this demonstration of divine power that would eventually prompt the Egyptians to thrust out their Hebrew slaves with such insistent urgings as to offer gifts of gold, silver and anything else a Hebrew might request. These slaves left the land with four hundred years' salary in their hands, making them wealthy beyond belief—which was in itself no small miracle.

This first encounter with the almighty God so changed Joshua that he was never the same again, and this has been the testimony of countless others who have experienced a measure of the energy of almighty God. How can anyone be the same after seeing God at work?

Today a far more cruel taskmaster than the Egyptians grasps control of men and women at an early age. Satan is a harsh slave driver, and he is no more eager to release an individual from his kingdom to worship God than was Egypt's Pharaoh. But the power of God is the same today as it was when Joshua was observing it. God still releases persons from the bonds and fetters of sin and brings them out of the kingdom of darkness into the kingdom of light.

Across this globe is a vast multitude of individuals who have been miraculously delivered from their "Egypt." Drunkards, drug addicts, licentious men and prostituting women, blasphemers, thieves and countless others who have been held captive by their pride, religion, passions, possessions, education, positions and other enslaving forces that prevented them from worshipping God have been set free by God's divine power. To them, their release is no less glorious than the release enjoyed by the Hebrews in Joshua's day. All have been set free to worship the living God. Paul, who experienced a dynamic release from religious bigotry, wrote, "For I am not ashamed of the gospel of Christ, for it is the power of God to salvation for everyone who believes, for the Jew first and also for the Greek'' (Rom. 1:16).

After the death of his oldest son, Pharaoh finally submitted to God's demands to release the Hebrews, and Joshua helped organize the exodus from Egypt. Quite understandably, the people wanted to bring everything they owned with them. After observing the Passover, the people set out with their young and aged, their flocks and herds and their tools and household implements, plus the great wealth taken from the Egyptians. They left with songs and shouts, for this was the most joyful occasion any of them had ever experienced. Joshua tried to establish some semblance of order in their march, but the people had not yet learned to function as a unit. They were certainly a motley crew, but they were free at last!

At the Red Sea, the people set up camp and rested amidst their rejoicing. Pharaoh, however, repented that he had released his workforce, and led his crack charioteers in pursuit of the Hebrews. The sound of running horses and whirling chariot wheels sent panic through the people, and they cried to Moses, "Let us alone that we may serve the Egyptians" (Ex. 14:12). But God had not brought them this far to abandon them to their former way of life. At God's command, "Moses stretched out his hand over the sea, and the Lord caused the sea to go back by a strong east wind all that night, and made the sea into dry land, and the waters were divided" (Ex. 14:21).

Joshua was incredulous. Never before in the history of the world had anything like this ever happened. The people were fearful to march between the towering walls of water, but when the Egyptian chariot charge began, they hastily changed their minds and followed Moses and Joshua through the sea to the other shore. There they watched with astonishment as the waters came together behind them—just as the last Hebrew stepped out of the sea bed and the rear guard of the Egyptian force stepped into it. The entire army was destroyed in a moment of time. This enemy would forever be powerless to oppress them again.

Paul wrote that ''all were baptized into Moses in the cloud and in the sea'' (1 Cor. 10:2), thus placing this miracle as a type of water baptism in which we are baptized into Christ Jesus. As surely as the crossing of the Red Sea forever severed these Hebrews from their former way of life, so water baptism performs a severance from our old walk and becomes an entrance to a new way of living. It is interesting that in India there is no prohibition against becoming a Christian, but national law revokes the citizenship of anyone who is baptized. Perhaps the enemy understands the rite of water baptism better than we, for all over the world it is the act of water baptism that serves as the absolute sign that the participant has renounced his former religion and has embraced Christ and Christianity.

Throughout the entire canon of the Old Testament, this miracle would be used as a measurement of the power of the omnipotent God, and it would remain as the outstanding demonstration of divine power until God raised Jesus from the dead. To his dying day, Joshua never forgot this display of Jehovah's might; he drew on it repeatedly to stir his faith to believe that God would intervene in situations he faced as Israel's leader.

Joshua Partook of God's Power
The logistics of leading this vast array of people

through the wilderness were mind-boggling to Joshua. (Note: Adam Clarke, the English commentator, estimates that from three to four million people came out.) The amount of bread needed for one day's ration would fill at least ten modern full-length freight trains; the water supply required was incalculable. But God provided manna every morning for forty years, and He opened the rock to gush forth water in such abundance as to satisfy both the people and their cattle. This was not a one-time demonstration of the power of almighty God; it happened every day until the miracles actually became commonplace and expected.

All who have followed the almighty God out of their "Egypts" into the wilderness of God's provision have discovered that the wilderness with God is preferred to the promised land without God, for in God's presence every longing is fulfilled. As Paul told the church at Philippi, "My God shall supply all your need according to His riches in glory by Christ Jesus" (Phil. 4:19). So faithfully and consistently does God provide for health, protection, food, clothing and shelter that the provision often becomes commonplace to us and we tend to think that we ourselves are the source of these things. God demonstrates His power so naturally that we fail to see the supernatural intervention that occurs.

But provision was not God's only demonstration of power for these Hebrews; God also revealed His power to protect what was His. Right after God opened the rock at Rephidim to supply water for the camp, Amalek brought his army to fight with Israel. To everyone's amazement, Moses chose Joshua to lead Israel's ragtag army against this formidable foe. These Hebrews were trained brickmakers and construction men, but they had never held a sword in their hands until they stripped the bodies of the Egyptians that washed up on the shores of the Red Sea. It looked like a suicide mission, but God gloriously intervened, and "Joshua defeated Amalek and his people with the edge of the sword" (Ex. 17:13). Joshua would long savor this victory over a superior foe by a greatly inferior army, and forty years later these memories would remind him that God delivers not by the might of soldiers but by the almightiness of His own divine nature.

David understood this protective power in God, for he wrote, "For the Lord Most High is awesome; He is a great King over all the earth. He will subdue the peoples under us, and the nations under our feet" (Ps. 47:2,3). In all of his conquests David credited God with victory, knowing full well that without divine intervention, Israel would often have seen defeat.

Cannot we trust this same almighty God to defend us in time of trouble? The unchangeable, omnipotent God still stands as a bulwark of defense for His people. Doesn't Isaiah testify to us, "When the enemy comes in like a flood, the Spirit of the Lord will lift up a standard against him" (Is. 59:19)? We may have even less fighting ability than untrained Joshua had, but God's power has never been limited by man's impotence.

But there was still more of God's almightiness to be demonstrated to Joshua, who was among the seventy elders who joined Moses, Aaron, Nadab and Abihu on the mountain: "And they saw the God of Israel. And there was under His feet as it were a paved work of sapphire stone, and it was like the very heavens in its clarity. But on the nobles of the children of Israel He did not lay His hand. So they saw God, and they ate and drank'' (Ex. 24:10,11).

From this experience of seeing and feasting with God, ''Moses arose with his assistant Joshua, and Moses went up to the mountain of God'' (Ex. 24:13). Scholars assumed that Joshua stayed at the outer fringes of the cloud of God's presence while Moses went into the very heart of it, but even so, Joshua would have been closer to God than anyone else in the camp except Moses.

It is not beyond the realm of probability that Joshua actually heard the voice of God talking to Moses. What a faith-building experience—to be an eavesdropper to the giving of the Law. Joshua so learned of God's power to communicate with humanity during the years that he served Moses that he had no difficulty discerning God's voice following the death of Moses.

God desires that all of His children feast with Him and enter into His presence and hear His voice. The promise of the final book of the Bible is ''Behold, I stand at the door and knock. If anyone hears My voice and opens the door, I will come in to him and dine with him, and he with Me'' and ''The Spirit and the bride say, 'Come!' And let him who hears say, 'Come!' And let him who thirsts come. And whoever desires, let him take the water of life freely'' (Rev. 3:20; 22:17). When we share fellowship in eating and drinking with God— feasting on Jesus—we discover that the power of God is not impersonal. God Himself is both the Almighty and our loving Father. Some people see only the power of God, while others accept an introduction to the person of God.

Again and again God displayed His almighty power to the Hebrews during their wilderness wanderings. He kept their clothing from wearing out for over forty years, gave them divine health, provided quail in great abundance when they murmured against the manna, and even healed them from the bites of the poisonous serpents. Joshua enjoyed—and participated in—forty years of continuous display of God's omnipotence. Joshua's knowledge wasn't theoretical, but practical. He could say with David, "He who dwells in the secret place of the Most High shall abide under the shadow of the Almighty" (Ps. 91:1).

Joshua Participated in God's Power

If anyone ever learned to "abide under the shadow of the Almighty," it was Joshua. Chosen by God to be successor to Moses, he was assured that "the Lord, He is the one who goes before you. He will be with you, He will not leave you nor forsake you; do not fear nor be dismayed" (Deut. 31:8). Apparently in the sight of all Israel, "Moses had laid his hands on him; so the children of Israel heeded him, and did as the Lord had commanded Moses" (Deut. 34:9). It seems Joshua was sworn in, much like a vice president is after the death of a U.S. president. Immediately Joshua felt the full mantle of authority and power descend upon him. He did not have a chance to grow into it, as Moses had; he entered it in a single day.

Joshua was still struggling with the tremendous weight of responsibility as Moses' replacement when an even heavier load was laid upon him. As soon as the thirty days of mourning for Moses ended, God spoke to Joshua, saying, "Moses My servant is dead. Now therefore, arise, go over this Jordan, you and all this people, to the land which I am giving to them—the children of Israel. Every place that the sole of your foot will tread upon I have given you, as I said to Moses'' (Josh. 1:2,3). From that moment on, Joshua was not merely filling the shoes of Moses; he was being commissioned to do the very thing that God had refused to allow Moses to do: lead the Hebrews into the promised land. This new leader was given a new vision, and accompanying that vision was God's assurance that ''as I was with Moses, so I will be with you'' (Josh. 1:5; 3:7). To assure Joshua that the people would follow him into this new venture, God told him, ''This day I will begin to magnify you in the sight of all Israel, that they may know that, as I was with Moses, so I will be with you'' (Josh. 3:7)

If Joshua expected God to be with him in the same *manner* He had been with Moses, Joshua was in for a great disappointment. Joshua did not have a burning bush experience when he was commissioned; he had to accept his commission through Moses. When God did speak to him directly, Joshua was instructed to do something that Moses never had done. And when crossing the Jordan River (which was to convince the people that God was with Joshua in the same *measure* that He had been with Moses), the method called for was entirely different from that used in crossing the Red Sea. Moses had been instructed to stretch forth his rod, but Joshua was told to have the priests bearing the ark of the covenant walk into the flooding river. How much easier it seems to learn God's methods than to know His voice. Joshua would have been comfortable stretching out a rod over the waters, but instead he had to convince the priests that their lives would not be endangered by walking into the river. The almighty God never runs out of creative ideas, and He seems to keep pulling them out of His hat—if for no other reason than to make us depend upon Him rather than on our memory of how He worked last month or last year. God is predictable as to His person but is frequently very unpredictable as to His performance. What worked in one service to bring an awareness of the presence of God may never work again.

The miracle of crossing the Jordan River was dynamic, as the cascading waters suddenly ceased at the very moment the feet of the priests entered the river, and "about forty thousand prepared for war crossed over before the Lord for battle, to the plains of Jericho. On that day the Lord magnified Joshua in the sight of all Israel; and they feared him, as they had feared Moses, all the days of his life" (Josh. 4:13,14). Although the method differed, the result was the same: dry passage and a reverential respect for the leader.

This display of the power of God may have produced faith in Joshua and veneration in the Hebrews, but it generated a fear and dread in the Amorites and the Canaanites, for when they "heard that the Lord had dried up the waters of the Jordan from before the children of Israel...their heart melted; and there was no spirit in them any longer because of the children of Israel" (Josh. 5:1). Our omnipotent God can and does use one display of might to accomplish many things. When God is allowed to move in His church on earth in a way that is consistent with His almighty nature, His work produces faith among the leadership, induces respect in the people and reduces the enemy to terror.

This was evident in the early church after the initial outpouring of the Holy Spirit and especially after God's judgment of Ananias and Sapphira, for we read, "So great fear came upon all the church and upon all who heard these things. And through the hands of the apostles many signs and wonders were done among the people... yet none of the rest dared join them, but the people esteemed them highly'' (Acts 5:11-13). Our efforts do not create apprehension in the people of the community; the manifested power of God does it automatically. We may formulate many substitutes for God's presence among us, but we can never find a replacement for the power of almighty God. While ceremony, pageantry, ritual, liturgy and litany may meet soulish or even spiritual needs in Christians, they can never take the place of God's demonstrated power to change the minds of unbelievers. When presenting God's word to people, one parted Jordan is worth ten thousand religious observances. As Job declared, ''With God is awesome majesty. As for the Almighty, we cannot find Him; He is excellent in power...Therefore men fear Him'' (Job 37:22-24).

The Conquest of the Promised Land

When Joshua found himself on the far side of the Jordan River, he needed every bit of understanding of the almighty God that he had gleaned over the forty years he had served Moses. The land, although promised by God to the Hebrews, was possessed by aliens who had to be driven out before it could be inhabited by God's chosen people. In God's sight, those aliens may have been usurpers, but in Joshua's estimation they were occupants. God had promised Israel a ''land flowing with milk and honey,'' but He hadn't bothered to mention that someone else owned the cows and the bees. Joshua's commission was to destroy these farmers without destroying their farms.

How often we Christians cringe in fear at the enemy

who holds possession of areas in life that God has promised to us, the overcomers. The milk and the honey seem enticing, but we don't want to battle the present inhabitants of the land. Victorious Christian living requires vicious spiritual battling, for we have the world, the flesh and the devil to overcome if we are ever to be possessors of God's great promises to us. To young Timothy, Paul wrote, ''But you, O man of God, flee these things and pursue righteousness, godliness, faith, love, patience, gentleness. Fight the good fight of faith, lay hold on eternal life, to which you were also called and have confessed the good confession in the presence of many witnesses'' (1 Tim. 6:11,12), and he reminded the church in Ephesus that ''we do not wrestle against flesh and blood, but against principalities, against powers, against the rulers of the darkness of this age, against spiritual hosts of wickedness in the heavenly places'' (Eph. 6:12). Fortunately, however, ''the weapons of our warfare are not carnal but mighty in God for pulling down strongholds, casting down arguments and every high thing that exalts itself against the knowledge of God, bringing every thought into captivity to the obedience of Christ'' (2 Cor. 10:4,5).

Joshua did not have this passage of Scripture to read, but he saw the dynamic truth of it unfolding before him day by day as he led Israel into battle after battle, though never into defeat. Every battle was different, and God's method of achieving victory in each battle was unique: Jericho was taken by disciplined marching around its walls for seven days followed by exuberant shouting at Joshua's command (see Josh. 6), but Ai was captured by use of an ambush (see Josh. 8). Later when Joshua had to defend the deceitful Gibeonites against an attack of a coalition of five kings, God intervened with giant hailstones that destroyed the opposing armies (see Josh. 10). As He revealed Himself as a God of infinite variety, He kept the enemy from figuring out an acceptable plan of defense. And, since no offensive pattern ever developed, no individual could ever take the credit for any of the victories.

As opposed to the Book of Judges, the Book of Joshua does not hail any heroes. One would expect to find a national image emerging from so successful a conquest, but even Joshua is not pictured as the glorious conqueror that the judges of a succeeding generation would be. Perhaps it stems from his confrontation with the "Lord of hosts" right after they crossed Jericho. Joshua "lifted his eyes and looked, and behold, a Man stood opposite him with His sword drawn in His hand. And Joshua went to Him and said to Him, 'Are You for us or for our adversaries?' So He said, 'No, but as Commander of the army of the Lord I have now come' " (Josh. 5:13,14). From that day on, Joshua did not consider himself as the commander-in-chief of Israel's army but as an officer who took orders from his superior.

To Israel, the promised land was not won by them—it was a gift of God. Unlike most epics, which love details of mighty deeds and battles, the biblical references to the conquest give little emphasis on particular battles; there are no human heroes or heroic acts mentioned as there were under Moses in the trans-Jordan battles against Sihon and Og. In the conquest of Canaan there is one hero, and only one: the almighty God Himself, and Israel gave Him all the glory and praise. Never in any of the writings of the poets or prophets is the conquest of this land spoken of as the result of the bravery of Joshua and his men; it is always seen as the gift of God. As a matter of fact, Joshua isn't even listed among the heroes of faith in the eleventh chapter of Hebrews, although we are told that "by faith the walls of Jericho fell down after they were encircled for seven days" (Heb. 11:30).

When Joshua sensed that his death was imminent, he called the elders of Israel together and challenged them to "choose for yourselves this day whom you will serve...." So the people answered and said: 'Far be it from us that we should forsake the Lord to serve other gods; for the Lord our God is He who brought us and our father up out of the land of Egypt, from the house of bondage, who did those great signs in our sight, and preserved us in all the way that we went and among all the people through whom we passed. And the Lord drove out from before us all the people, even the Amorites who dwelt in the land. We also will serve the Lord, for He is our God' " (Josh. 24:15-18). It was the demonstrated power of the almighty God that formed the basis of their unchanging faith, and it was lasting, for we read, "Israel served the Lord all the days of Joshua, and all the days of the elders who outlived Joshua, who had known all the works of the Lord which He had done for Israel" (Josh. 24:31).

Seeing the Almighty God Inspires Worship

Since the depth of our revelation of God determines our response to God, it is imperative that we be introduced to the almighty God. Shallow experiences produce shallow faith that often fails with the passage of time. In his book *Whatever Happened to Worship?* A.W. Tozer makes this observation: "If there is to be true and blessed worship, some things in your life must be destroyed, eliminated. The gospel of Jesus Christ is certainly positive and constructive. But it must be destructive in some areas, dealing with and destroying certain elements that cannot remain in a life pleasing to God.''

Each of us needs a deliverance from ''Egypt''; we need to leave some things behind when we begin to follow the omnipotent God. Furthermore, there will be dealings of God during the entire period of wilderness training, and we must have the overcoming power of God in our lives on a day-to-day basis. None of this comes as a result of mere discipline or self-determination; it is a by-product of walking in holy communion with the almighty God. Peter said of God, ''His divine power has given to us all things that pertain to life and godliness, through the knowledge of Him who called us by glory and virtue, by which have been given to us exceedingly great and precious promises, that through these you may be partakers of the divine nature, having escaped the corruption that is in the world through lust'' (2 Pet. 1:3,4). We need not do what He has done, but we must relate to Him so that He can apply it to our lives. The power of God that was exhibited in the days of Joshua is unchanged today, for we do not have one God of the Old Testament and another God of the New Testament. ''There is no other God but one'' (1 Cor. 8:4). This God, revealed as Jehovah in the Old Testament and as Christ Jesus in the New Testament, is unchangeable in His nature, for ''Jesus Christ is the same yesterday, today, and forever'' (Heb. 13:8).

Since God is referred to as the almighty God in both the Old and the New Testaments, and since He is always the same, His power is as available to the church today as it was to Israel in the days of Joshua. The cleansing power of the blood of Jesus Christ still reaches to the vilest sinner. The overcoming power of the Word of God continues to lead Christians into victory. The indwelling power of the Holy Spirit is as real at this hour as it was on the day of Pentecost, and the healing power of Christ Jesus is still available for the sick and the suffering. It is not God who has changed; our concept of God has degenerated from that of the almighty God to a limited God whose abilities are barely above our own.

Daniel proclaimed, "The people who know their God shall be strong, and carry out great exploits" (Dan. 11:32). For a lengthy lifetime Joshua served and worshipped God because he met a God whose self-revelation to him was progressively higher until he came to know a full measure of God's almightiness. Can we continue worshipping God with a lesser vision of Him? The elders in heaven seemed to need this concept of God, for, having prostrated themselves before Him, they worshipped Him, saying, "We give You thanks, O Lord God Almighty, the One who is and who was and who is to come, because You have taken Your great power and reigned" (Rev. 11:17).

It will take a concept of God's mighty power for us to stand with Isaiah and meet a holy God and still be able to worship Him.

chapter six

ISAIAH MET A HOLY GOD

"...our God is holy."
(Psalm 99:9)

There are few Christians who are unfamiliar with Isaiah's confrontation with a holy God, for the cry of one seraphim to the other has not only become the theme of many of our hymns but is often the prayer of the Spirit within our lives: "Holy, holy, holy is the Lord of hosts; the whole earth is full of His glory!" (Is. 6:3). It seems that the two attributes of God that overawed and overwhelmed these supernatural beings are God's holiness and His omnipotence. His holiness is His inner glory, while His omnipotence is His outer glory. He is holy, holy, holy inwardly—perfectly, unspeakably, uncompromisingly holy—and then outwardly, the whole earth is full of His glory—everything in creation expresses His glory and becomes the garment by which He is made visible.

The imprint of the cry of the seraphim lasted Isaiah for a lifetime, and throughout his lengthy book he used two separate names for God. To denote the holiness of God, he called Him the "Holy One of Israel," and to designate the omnipotence of God, he called Him "the Lord of hosts."

It is likely that we must come to the omnipotence of the almighty God before we can come to His holiness; because we are mentally qualified to proceed from the known to the unknown, from the visible to the invisible, we can appreciate God's demonstration of Himself more easily than we can comprehend His essential nature. Joshua knew an omnipotent God by the successive demonstrations of His power, but Isaiah was destined to come into a further revelation of God: a vision of His holiness.

Isaiah's Vision of the Throne Room

Isaiah himself told us the circumstances behind his vision of the Lord in saying, "In the year that King Uzziah died, I saw the Lord" (Is. 6:1). While most of the Old Testament prophets were of humble origins, Isaiah was of the nobility. He was an accepted statesman who had access to the palace and to the king. During his lifetime he was spiritual advisor to four kings in Judah. Many writers express the opinion that Isaiah was a cousin of King Uzziah, who was only sixteen years old when he ascended the throne. Uzziah, one of Judah's better kings, reigned for fifty-two years. The Bible tells us some of the main achievements of his reign, and, although he ended his years as a leper because of God's judgment upon him for presuming to do the office of a priest in burning incense in the holy place, as long as he sought after God, he enjoyed the blessing of God.

Uzziah's death caused a season of national mourning, and Isaiah went to the temple looking for consolation.

How often it takes a sorrow or tragedy to motivate us to seek solace in God. Very frequently God has to allow our "Uzziahs" to pass from the scene so that we will look away from our earthly "kings" and see the "King of kings." Isaiah could no longer come into the presence of the king of Judah, but he now found himself in the presence of the ultimate King, the One who sat forever on the throne of Judah. He saw the Lord. It was far more than a fair exchange, and it will always be a bonus for us to exchange an earthly relationship for a heavenly one. What we see with our natural eyes is often our greatest barrier to spiritual vision.

In the midst of his personal sorrow and the uncertainty of what the reign of Uzziah's son, Jotham, would bring, Isaiah was confronted with a glimpse into the heavens. "I saw the Lord sitting on a throne," he wrote. Our translators use the lower case for the word "Lord," for the name of God used here is *Adonai*, which means "sovereign One." Technically it is not the name of God; it is a title for God. When "Lord" appears in all capital letters it indicates that the word *Yahweh* is being translated. *Jehovah*, as the King James Version transliterates the Hebrew, is the sacred, unspeakable, ineffable name that was considered so holy by the Jews that they would not pronounce it. Normally it occurs only with the use of its four consonants—*yhwh*. Theologians refer to this as the "tetragrammaton," the unspeakable four letters. "LORD" is the name of God; "Lord" is His title. Isaiah was presented to the "sovereign One," much as a dignitary might be presented to the president of the United States or to the queen of England. Their title precedes their name, just as their office exceeds their personage. Worried about an earthly potentate,

Isaiah was presented before the *Adoni* of heaven—the sovereign LORD.

This great One, whose face may not be seen, was "sitting on a throne." This is, of course, consistent with the title of the One on the throne—sovereign—but it probably spoke to Isaiah of far more than mere authority. The only seat in the tabernacle, and later in the temple, was the mercy seat, which all Israel visualized as the throne of God among them. It functioned as the propitiatory, and it was Israel's assurance of God's forgiveness of confessed sins. In the New Testament, God's throne is not pictured as a place so awesome that we dread to approach it; instead, we are told, "Let us therefore come boldly to the throne of grace, that we may obtain mercy and find grace to help in time of need" (Heb. 4:16). Isaiah was not brought before the judgment seat of Christ; he stood before the mercy seat of the almighty God.

The throne, and its occupant, were "high and lifted up," for even in the heaven of heavens there is nothing above the omnipotent, holy God. When Lucifer said, "I will exalt my throne above the stars of God...I will be like the Most High" (Is. 14:13,14), he was cast out of heaven, for none can ever equal, much less be exalted above, our God. Every time the Bible gives us a glimpse into heaven, we see the triune God exalted above everything else described. When God raised Christ from the dead, He "seated Him at His right hand in the heavenly places, far above all principality and power and might and dominion, and every name that is named, not only in this age but also in that which is to come. And He put all things under His feet, and gave Him to be head over all things to the church, which is His body, the fullness of Him who fills all in all'' (Eph. 1:20,23). Isaiah stood in the presence of the most exalted Lord God, who said, ''There is no other God besides Me, a just God and a Savior; there is none besides Me (Is. 45:21).

Isaiah's Vision of God

Isaiah's vision of God included the great spiritual beings who surround the throne. These divine attendants who proclaim God's holiness bear a marked resemblance to the living creatures of Revelation, who also have six wings and ''do not rest day or night, saying: 'Holy, holy, holy, Lord God Almighty, Who was and is and is to come!' '' (Rev. 4:8). Isaiah calls them ''seraphim,'' which means ''fiery ones.'' Since this title is not used elsewhere in the Bible, some scholars believe that the ''seraphim'' of Isaiah and the ''cherubim'' of Ezekiel are the same as the ''living creatures'' of Revelation. Others feel that we are given fleeting glimpses of three orders of spiritual intelligences, resembling each other, yet distinct. God accommodates our limited capacity to comprehend the spirit world by giving us symbolic terms and descriptions of these beings; a literal description would be as unintelligible to us as a comprehensive explanation of a computer would be to a member of a lost tribe in Borneo.

The heart of Isaiah's revelation is the cry of these seraphim: ''Holy, holy, holy is the Lord of hosts.'' It is the holiness of God that becomes their subject of adoration and song. The attributes of the Most High are the themes of their thought and worship, but it is God's holiness that excites their most rapturous praise. Since they have never needed His mercy, they do not sing of redemption; they magnify the holiness which has been shown in God's great redemption of mankind. All God's other attributes and actions are valuable only because they are directed by unswerving holiness. God's holiness is the foundation of the peace, the joy and the love of the moral universe.

Three times they chant "holy." No other characteristic of God is ever repeated three times. Never do we read of the angelic hosts crying, "Omnipotent, omnipotent, omnipotent is the Lord of hosts," nor does the Bible say, "God is love, love, love," but twice in scriptural glimpses into heaven we hear these magnificent ministers unto God declare, "Holy, holy, holy is the Lord of hosts" (see Is. 6:3; Rev. 4:8). In both the Hebrew and Greek languages repetition is often used for emphasis. Jesus used this form of emphasis in saying, "Verily, verily," or "Truly, truly I say unto you...," and it signified that what He was about to say was of vital importance. Undoubtedly the angels in heaven use the Hebrew poetic form of emphasis by repetition to establish the certainty or importance of His holiness. God is holy, and this truth cannot be overemphasized either in heaven or on earth.

It is distinctly possible that the seraphim declared God to be holy three times because they were expressing the holiness of the triune God. While "the Lord our God, the Lord is one!" (Deut. 6:4), He has chosen to manifest Himself in three persons: Father, Son and Holy Spirit. Perhaps the seraphim were saying, "Holy Father, Holy Son, Holy Spirit," for in the barest minimum God is essentially thrice holy.

Accurately and fully defining holy is a task beyond my ability. The first word that comes to mind as a synonym is purity, and while that is implied, it is certainly not equivalent to holy. Theologians, who are more practiced than most of us in defining the nature of God, use the word transcendence to describe the holiness of God. The Merriam-Webster Seventh New Collegiate Dictionary defines transcend as "exceeding usual limits: surpassing; extending or lying beyond the limits of ordinary experience." When the Bible calls God holy, it fundamentally means that God is transcendentally separate, that He is above and beyond us, and that in His exalted loftiness and consuming majesty He is separated by an infinite distance from every creature. If our sinful eyes could read spiritual symbols, we would see, on all sides of the throne room, signs bearing the familiar words "Keep Out." In His infinite holiness God has no place for sinful people.

If God's holiness is ignored or forgotten, we create the concept of a sentimental, indulgent divine love which makes the gospel unnecessary and wastes the very blood of Christ. The heart of the gospel lies in the reality that the unapproachable God Himself has provided a way of access through Christ Jesus our Lord. When God, in the form of Jesus, came to earth, the transcendent God bridged the distance between His holiness and eternity and our unholy time-space capsule. He made Himself available to lowly people.

This, of course, defies the intellect of the world's wisest persons, but through Isaiah, God said, " 'For My thoughts are not your thoughts, nor are your ways My ways,' says the Lord. 'For as the heavens are higher than the earth, so are My ways higher than your ways, and My thoughts than your thoughts' " (Is. 55:8,9).

Holiness is a glorious perfection belonging to the

nature of God. The Bible does not speak of His mighty name or His wise name but rather of His holy name. Negatively, God's holiness is a perfect and unpolluted freedom from all evil. There is absolutely nothing unholy in Him. Positively, His holiness is the perfection, purity and absolute sanctity of His nature. It is the integrity of the divine nature. His holiness is as necessary as His being or His omniscience. As He is God from eternity, so He is holy from eternity, and only God is absolutely holy, for the Bible declares, "There is none holy like the Lord" (1 Sam. 2:2). This holiness fills not only the heaven of heavens but also the whole earth, for the proclamation was "The whole earth is full of His glory!"

Some theologians speak of holiness as the pervading moral attribute of God's nature. Others insist that it is not one attribute among the other attributes but is the innermost reality to which all others are related. Either way, they are far from accurate in describing God's holiness as an attribute, as they might speak of His omnipotence or His love. Why? Because throughout the Scriptures the word "holy" is used as a synonym for His deity and as a part of His name. Holy calls attention to all God is: His love is holy love, His mercy is holy mercy, and His Spirit is the Holy Spirit. To say that God is holy is to describe His essence, not His attributes.

Volume 2 of The Interpreter's Dictionary of the Bible says, "Even the sum of all the attributes and activities of the holy is insufficient to exhaust its meaning, for to the one who has experienced its presence there is always a plus, a 'something more,' which resists formulation or definition. Its connotations are as diverse as the cultures which seek to describe its mysterious nature, but common to all is an awareness of an undefined and uncanny energy, a sense...of the imponderable and incomprehensible, an inarticulate feeling of inviolable potency outside and beyond, removed and distant, yet at the same time near and 'fascinating,' invading the everyday world of normal experience."

In my earlier book *Let Us Be Holy*, I wrote, "Sometimes when the Scriptures speak of holiness it is used in a moral sense, and other times it has little ethical connotation. Whatever was devoted to God and His service was declared 'holy' whether it be people ('holy prophets'), property ('holy ark') or places ('holy city'). This did not necessarily signify that they were partakers of God's nature, but that they had been separated unto His use. They were holy because they belonged to the Holy One.

"When the context signifies that a moral or ethical sense is intended we gain a far greater insight into the meaning of holiness, for usually the accompanying passage includes words and phrases that help to define, explore, and enlarge our concept of holiness. These give us both color and contrast, and express the positive and negative factors in holiness. Trying to explain holiness without these verbal shades of meaning is akin to trying to describe the beauty of a sunset by using only the words 'black and white.' "

Since there is nothing on earth that compares with God, our concepts of Him fall far short of reality. When He reveals an area of His majestic holiness, we are filled with a sense of wonder not too unlike that which the man born blind must have experienced when he saw the face of Jesus, his healer.

MEETING GOD

All attempts to define God meet with frustration. Godly scholars throughout the ages have sought to reduce God's limited revelation of Himself to a creed or statement of faith. But when the best minds have finished their search and the most adept writers have reduced those concepts to carefully chosen words, a tremendous mystery remains; our holy God is easier to experience than to explain. Isaiah felt that mystery and responded to it almost immediately.

Isaiah's Vision of Himself

"Woe is me, for I am undone!" he cried. There are at least three views of each of us: the way others see us, the way God sees us and the way we see ourselves. From our perspective in history we see Isaiah as a learned writer, a statesman, a reformer, the greatest of the prophets, a teacher, the outstanding theologian of the Old Testament and a martyr—for legend has it that he was placed inside a hollow tree and sawn asunder at the command of Manasseh (see Heb. 11:37).

God saw Isaiah as a man with a heart after Him. God had watched Isaiah's response to an earlier call to the prophetic office and He saw faithfulness and consistency. There was, however, a defilement in Isaiah that weakened God's message through him. God knew that He could easily remove this if Isaiah would consent, so God brought His prophet into a direct confrontation with the Holy One of Israel.

Whenever we see God, we will inevitably see ourselves. During this divine confrontation, Isaiah saw himself differently from the way he had ever seen himself before. In contrast to his contemporaries, Isaiah was a holy man of God, but in comparison to God he was an "undone man." It was not the sight of God that undid him, for that was beautiful and exhilarating; it was seeing himself measured alongside God that devastated him, for unholiness is never more evident than when in the presence of absolute holiness. Those who have never had a sense of their own vileness are always destitute of a sense of God's holiness.

Isaiah's cry, "Woe is me, for I am undone!" (Is. 6:5), is almost lost to our generation. Isaiah was already a commissioned prophet of Yahweh and he was accustomed to giving a divine message which was generally called the "oracle." These oracles were merely announcements from God, whether they were good news or bad news. The "good news" oracles generally began with the word "blessed," as Christ stated in the Beatitudes, but the "bad news" oracles began with the word "woe." Jesus used this introductory form when He spoke to the Pharisees, and Isaiah used it more than twenty times in his book. Isaiah was here declaring a negative oracle upon himself in saying, "Woe is me...I am a man of unclean lips." Isaiah, the scholar, well knew that the provision of the Law required the leper to cover his lips and declare himself, "Unclean! Unclean!" (see Lev. 13:45). King Uzziah had been reduced to the level of that confession for violating the sanctity of God's house; but now the prophet had gazed on a holier sanctuary, in which the King of glory was enthroned, and the sight had stricken him with the sense of his spiritual leprosy. Does any one of us escape the feeling of uncleanness when brought into the presence of a holy God? Even the seraphim covered their faces with two of their wings, as though even their powerful words of adoration were unclean compared to the majestic holiness of the almighty God.

There may very well be a second reason that Isaiah wailed, "I am a man of unclean lips, and I dwell in the midst of a people of unclean lips" (Is. 6:5). His consciousness of defilement centered on his speech: something was wrong with his mouth.

Some have suggested this cry to be a confession of the use of profanity, but that seems highly unlikely, as it would have been a confession of something he had done rather than of what he actually was. It is far more probable that Isaiah, like Moses before him when meeting God at the burning bush, felt totally incapable of speaking on God's behalf once he had truly met God. Isaiah had a strong consciousness of inefficiency and ineptness, as though none of his past training or experience was sufficient for his present calling. Isaiah was being reduced to total dependency upon the Lord.

As long as God leaves anything in us upon which we can lean, we seldom rely on Him, so He purposefully strips us of all self-sufficiency. Isaiah's experience is a typical one, and it was recorded for our edification and admonition. The person who has never felt unfit will never be fit for any great spiritual service. Jeremiah, at his call, felt that he was "a child"; Moses, that he was "slow of speech and slow of tongue"; John fell at the feet of the Son of man "as one dead," mind and hand paralyzed, before taking up the pen that glowed with apocalyptic fire. God need not choose "fit" persons; He chooses available persons and makes them fit by an encounter with His holy presence.

Isaiah not only saw himself as possessing unclean lips, but he declared that the people to whom he had been sent also had unclean lips. Perhaps he was pleading the overwhelming power of his environment; possibly he was admitting that he was no better than the very ones to whom he had been challenged to prophesy—for God does not call humans to teach angels and rarely consigns angels to teach humans. He chooses people to preach to people who are just like the messengers were before their call. He simply changes the hearts of His messengers before He commissions them.

God's equipping is consistent with His commissioning. Isaiah was to be the prophet of both the Lord's terror and His mercy. He was to denounce sin with the solemnity of one who knew God's thought of sin. Isaiah was to produce conviction of sin in the corrupt minds and hearts of the people, and he was to announce the coming of the great messenger of divine mercy. To do this, he had to have his own soul filled with the infinite glory and holiness of God; he had to have a humbling sense of sin. No one can minister what he has yet to experience. Like the Cushite, who was told to "Go, tell the king what you have seen" (2 Sam. 18:21), we have been commissioned to share what we have seen and experienced in Christ Jesus. Parrots can get by with repeating what they have heard others say; prophets are expected to see and to know for themselves.

The question today is not whether we have Isaiah's cleanness but whether we have his awareness of defilement. Our generation is so familiar with sin that they are unaware of it as such. Because television flashes such an endless variety of sin into our own homes, we have lost the horror of sin. We see it as the entertainment industry sees it, not as a holy God views it. We've become so dulled that depravity is now found within the circle of the just, among those who are called to be saints. Sin has closed their ears to God's voice and blinded their eyes to spiritual realities.

More than the harsh preaching of sin that so stirred people in past generations, our generation needs a confrontation with the holy God; just as the brilliance of the sun will reveal stains that are not seen in the moonlight, so the radiance of God's holiness will show us the depravity of our hearts even as our lips speak our devotion.

Much of our problem in maintaining fellowship with a holy God is that many Christians repent only for what they do rather than for what they are. Isaiah did not confess bad speaking; he confessed bad lips.

Once Isaiah's confession was complete, his cleansing began. He testified that "one of the seraphim flew to me, having in his hand a live coal which he had taken with the tongs from the altar. And he touched my mouth with it, and said: 'Behold, this has touched your lips; your iniquity is taken away, and your sin purged' " (Is. 6:6,7). All Isaiah needed to do was to confess his condition. Then everything was done for him, for no one can cleanse the least defilement from his or her own life. Isaiah was not cleansed by blood; he was purged by fire. The work of the brazen altar [the cross in the New Testament] was complete and did not need to be redone. This cleansing was effected by the application of fire from the golden altar of incense to the place of defilement in the prophet.

Today's Christians like to talk of Isaiah's vision and awareness, but they do not like to think of the fire-hot coal that was placed on the prophet's lips. They want to see what Isaiah saw, but they do not want to feel what he felt. As long as they hold this view they will be unable to minister as he did. Cleansing is not an option for the person who aspires to God's service. It is obligatory: no cleansing, no commission; no purging, no power. Defilement leads to disqualification. In writing to Timothy about the qualifications of leaders, Paul said, "Let everyone who names the name of Christ depart from iniquity...If anyone cleanses himself from the latter, he will be a vessel for honor, sanctified and useful for the Master, prepared for every good work" (2 Tim. 2:19,21).

It was at the place of worship, the golden altar, that Isaiah was purged from his iniquity, and the immediate result was "I heard the voice of the Lord" (Is. 6:8). Up until the time of his purging Isaiah could hear only the voice of the seraphim, but in his cleansed condition he clearly heard God speak (Is. 6:8). It is always our sins that separate us from God, as Isaiah later preached (see Is. 59:2). Much of our problem in maintaining fellowship with a holy God is that many Christians repent only for what they do rather than for what they are. Isaiah did not confess bad speaking; he confessed bad lips.

Because our God is holy, He is actively hostile to sin. God can only burn on and on against sin forever. Once our sin is purged and our lives have been purified by a coal from the altar of incense, our spiritual sensitivity is heightened to a point where we can see and hear things to which we were formerly blind and deaf. When we pray and ask God to open our spiritual ears, He often answers by applying a coal of fire to a very different part of our lives—for it is sin that has closed those ears, and God deals with sin wherever He finds it. When we stand in the place of worship as Isaiah stood, we can expect both the revelation and the removal of our sin.

This puts us in a grand position to worship the holy One seated upon the throne.

Once Isaiah's sin was removed, he lost consciousness of the temple, the train, the throne and the seraphim, and focused his entire attention upon God. He responded instantly to God's expressed desires, in short, he worshipped. Worship is responding to the holy God far more than it is reacting to His holiness. When God said, "Whom shall I send, and who will go for Us?," Isaiah immediately responded, "Here am I! Send me" (Is. 6:8).

Worship is not all song and dance; it is also submission to the divine will and service to the holy God. Heaven's greatest worshippers—the angels and the elders—are also God's greatest servants, involved with Him in all of His activities. I've heard of church staff members who, after meeting God, have such a desire to worship that they want to pray and "talk about Jesus" all day rather than work for Him. Sometimes pastors have had to replace formerly good workers because they could not channel their worship of God into work for God. Worship with our lips is wonderful and very scriptural, but it must be balanced with the worship of our lives. It should not be either/or; it should be both/and.

Worship is humanity's answer to God's voice and His person. It is the answer of our conscience—the answer of our hearts. We cannot worship until we come face to face with God, and then we cannot help worshipping, for no one in all the pages of the Holy Bible ever had a personal confrontation with God Himself without immediately responding in worship.

The real key to worship is not technique but revelation, and if our heavenly vision is dimmed, our worship will not be bright. If our ears are closed to hearing God's voice our voices will be stopped from melodious singing. If our wills are not wholly submitted to the divine will, our worship will be only a mockery of God, for in effect we will be saying to Him, "I love and adore You, but I do not choose to obey You."

When Isaiah's mouth was touched by the fiery coal, it became totally submitted to God's will. What wondrous praises flowed from that mouth in years to come. Listen to him worship:

"Praise the Lord, call upon His name; declare His deeds among the peoples, make mention that His name is exalted. Sing to the Lord, for He has done excellent things; this is known in all the earth. Cry out and shout, O inhabitant of Zion, for great is the Holy One of Israel in your midst!" (Is. 12:4-6).

"O Lord, You are my God. I will exalt You, I will praise Your name, for You have done wonderful things; Your counsels of old are faithfulness and truth" (Is. 25:1).

"The Lord is exalted, for He dwells on high; He has filled Zion with justice and righteousness. Wisdom and knowledge will be the stability of your times, and the strength of salvation; the fear of the Lord is His treasure" (Is. 33:5,6).

If, as we have stated, holiness is God's perfection and transcendence, then let us glorify this holiness of God. Moses glorified it in his writings and in his songs; the heavenly seraphim have their mouths filled with the praises of it. The saints, whether militant on earth or triumphant in heaven, are enjoined to continue the same acclamation of "Holy, holy, holy, Lord God Almighty"

(Rev. 4:8). Everything of God is glorious, but His holiness is the most glorious of all. If God built the world principally for anything, it was for the communication of His goodness and the display of His holiness. It is to be expected, then, that we, His redeemed creatures, would regularly, devotedly, lovingly, enthusiastically and even melodiously worship our holy God.

This is not merely our duty and pleasure while we are here on this earth; it will be our joy and chief occupation throughout all of eternity, for, as Ezekiel learned, God is a glorious God who is to be worshipped "world without end."

chapter seven

EZEKIEL MET THE GLORY OF GOD

"...the God of glory...."
(Psalm 29:3)

It was Ezekiel's birthday—his thirtieth birthday—the beginning of the year to which he had looked forward from his earliest memories. Born to the levitical priesthood, Ezekiel had probably started training for his life's work at about age twenty. According to the provision of the Law of Moses (see Num. 4:23,30) he was to have been consecrated to his ministry on this very birthday, but factors over which he had no control had changed his life completely. Although technically he was a priest from this day forward, actually he was a captive in Babylon, far removed from the temple and all of the rites and rituals he had been prepared to perform. He was not only a man without a country; he was a priest without a parish, possessing a title but no task.

We dare not impose our Western minds on Ezekiel's predicament, for his thought patterns were completely different from ours. Before the Babylonian captivity,

133

the Hebrews shared their neighbors' territorial concept of religion. Each people had its own god, and that god's jurisdiction was limited to the land which his people inhabited. For that reason, when Ruth the Moabitess chose to follow her mother-in-law back to Canaan, she exclaimed, "Your people shall be my people, and your God, my God" (Ruth 1:16). Orpah, on the other hand, is said to have "gone back to her people and to her gods" (Ruth 1:15). For people who thought in these terms, exile was a major disaster in both the religious and the political spheres. Ezekiel was not only removed from his homeland and its temple; he very likely felt cut off from his God as well. God was in the land He had given to His people under Joshua, but this priest was in a strange land as a prisoner of war.

We might pass off such religious concepts as unduly superstitious, but religion cannot live exclusively in a realm of ideas; it must have some visible status in this daily world, for the invisible church is known through the visible church on earth. With our inner religious experiences come attachments to particular places, persons, times and institutions. If these attachments are severed, our spiritual lives may be threatened. When families move from one location to another, they often seem to lose their spiritual relationship because in their minds they connect their God to the church where they were saved, baptized and perhaps married. Not everyone has developed a relationship with God that is sufficiently strong to survive the loss of old ties. Ezekiel was certainly witnessing this among the captives in Babylon. On this particular day, his own faith was tested to its limits. Was it possible that he was not only without an office, without a temple, without a sacrificial system, but also without a God?

The Glory Revealed

It is improbable that Ezekiel was a man who would question his faith, but he had questions *in* his faith, and those questions needed some answers. So on this day that was to have been the highlight of his life, he found a solitary place along the banks of the river Chebar and there he meditated on the storm that engulfed his life and his nation. Suddenly, "the word of the Lord came expressly to Ezekiel the priest, the son of Buzi...and the hand of the Lord was upon him there" (Ezek. 1:3). Jehovah's immediate response to the inner turmoil of Ezekiel was to give him a vision of a great whirlwind coming out of the north and a giant cloud "with raging fire engulfing itself" which was surrounded by radiant brightness that reminded him of molten brass being poured from the furnace (see Ezek. 1:4).

In this confrontation, in which Ezekiel's commission was changed from that of a priest to that of a prophet. Perhaps God was demonstrating a principle: anyone who wants to find Him in the midst of a threatening storm must begin by facing the storm at its most fierce; there is no revelation of God for those who shrink from their circumstances and calling. When Ezekiel confronted the storm cloud without flinching, he saw the glory of the Lord.

We, too, must learn to face our crises, whether in private or public life, with a valiant spirit. As we do so, the clouds will begin to glow with light, and the splendor of God will be unveiled before our eyes. We need to see God enthroned in majesty above all the forces of nature, above all the spirit forces that oppose us daily. Our circumstances may be distressingly negative, but our God has not withdrawn from us; He is present and is in complete control.

This is what God impressed upon Ezekiel during this vision, his prophetic commission. Now Ezekiel, the priest and prophet, could convince the captives in Babylon that, though they had lost land and temple, God remained. This prophet to the exiles was commissioned to show men and women an ever-present God who would go where they went and abide where they abode. David sang this truth in a song to his chief musician: "Where can I go from Your Spirit? Or where can I flee from Your presence? If I ascend into heaven, You are there; if I make my bed in hell, behold, You are there. If I take the wings of the morning, and dwell in the uttermost parts of the sea, even there Your hand shall lead me, and Your right hand shall hold me" (Ps. 139:7-10).

The truth of David's song had not always gripped the people of Ezekiel's generation, so God restated this truth in vision form during the commissioning of Ezekiel, who in turn taught it to the people through the prophetic gift. Succinctly put, Ezekiel's message was "Our captivity is God's answer to our sin of departure from God, but He is in our captivity, and He is with us in our captivity. Nothing is out of control, and God has not retreated into His heaven."

This first of many visions that Ezekiel would see involved an unusual storm, high-level angelic beings and a portable throne on which a "man" was seated. Ezekiel summarized the picture by saying, "This was the appearance of the likeness of the glory of the Lord" (Ezek. 1:28). Most of Ezekiel's written description focuses attention upon the cherubim with their four separate faces, six wings, human hands and wheels, but all Ezekiel could say of God was that He had human form and *"the appearance of fire"* (Ezek. 1:27, emphasis added). This was an incredibly bold statement for a Hebrew to make. To the Hebrews, Yahweh was invisible and therefore indescribable. Actually seeing God was considered a death warrant. Even so, Moses had declared that he saw God's "back"; Isaiah wrote that he "saw the Lord...high and lifted up"; and here Ezekiel opened the door a little further, saying he'd seen God in a human outline but with so dazzling a splendor that nothing more could be described. It would be left to Daniel to go even further and describe in detail the features of the Ancient of Days (see Dan. 7:9,10).

It was a deeply held tenet of the Hebrew religion from Moses until Christ that God could not be visibly expressed, and for that very reason idolatry was banned. But when God appeared as a theophany, it was the human form he chose to use to represent the deity. However, it was no mere human that Ezekiel saw, for His radiance was surrounded by the glory of a rainbow, and the prophet could only fall on his face in the dust before his God.

Ezekiel used all the resources of nature to express his representation of Jehovah as possessing unapproachable splendor. He showed the glory of the eternal in the living creatures, in human attributes, in intelligence and especially in divine utterance, but he failed, as all must fail, in the attempt to portray that which cannot be portrayed. Nothing is easier than to determine *that* God is, while nothing is more difficult than to describe *what* He is.

Ezekiel's language, glowing as it is, gives but hints and suggestions of glory that surpasses human comprehension. He candidly admitted that "this was the appearance of the likeness of the glory of the Lord" (Ezek. 1:28). But be it actuality or mere appearance, this self-manifestation of God, which Ezekiel called "the glory of God," so filled his mind that he spoke of it eleven times in the first eleven chapters of his book, and he mentioned it an additional five times in the closing chapters. When we add to this the statement "You shall know that I am the Lord," which Ezekiel made over sixty times, we cannot miss seeing that he was consumed with God's desire to reveal Himself to His people, even in the midst of their chastisement.

Ezekiel was unquestionably the prophet of God's glory. He saw it, he heard it and he felt it, and to his dying day no one could take his experience away from him. The appearance of God completely transformed him and ultimately consumed him. He had seen God, and nothing on earth mattered after that encounter.

The Glory Repeated

The word Ezekiel used for glory is *kabodh*, which denotes glory and honor but literally means "weight." From this Paul drew his concept of the "eternal weight of glory" (2 Cor. 4:17). In Ezekiel's secular world, *kabodh* would have been used to describe a man of substance or wealth. Such a man's external appearance would reflect his wealth and would also be called *kabodh*. His wealth and dignity demanded and compelled respect and honor from his companions, and that, too, was called *kabodh*. So weight, substance, wealth, dignity, noble bearing and honor all contributed to the meaning of this term. To these fundamental meanings Ezekiel added that of brightness. He saw outer demonstrations of God that revealed some of His inner being, and he called this "the glory of God."

This new concept of God culminated in Ezekiel's commission. As this first vision began to fade, the Spirit of God entered Ezekiel and spoke to him, saying, "Son of man, I am sending you to the children of Israel, to a rebellious nation that has rebelled against Me....I am sending you to them, and you shall say to them, 'Thus says the Lord God' " (Ezek. 2:3,4). Following this initial commission, Ezekiel was lifted up by the Spirit, and he heard "a great thunderous voice: 'Blessed is the glory of the Lord from His place!' " (Ezek. 3:12).

Deposited by the Spirit among the captives, Ezekiel sat both silent and astonished for seven days. The vision passed, but its power remained with the prophet, for the ecstasy of great spiritual experiences diminishes slowly. Ezekiel suddenly had a commission but, not yet knowing what to do with it, he sat for seven days among his fellow captives. Over and over again I've noticed that zeal for God becomes channeled when we are forced to be among people. If Ezekiel had remained apart from his people, his call would not have become clear to him. There is a time for withdrawal to the secret place with God, but there is also a time to return to normal activity with the people we have been commissioned to serve. Ezekiel saw the glory of the God of Israel, but he also saw the gloom of the people of Israel. Without the first, he had nothing to minister; without the second, he had no one to minister to, for a true prophet must see both God and the people.

Ezekiel was given a second vision of the glory of the Lord when his commission was expanded to cause him to be a physical demonstration to the people (see Ezek. 3:23-27). The Spirit of the Lord took the power of

139

speech from him. He could speak only when the glory of the Lord chose to speak through him in prophetic utterances, and he was given explicit details of how he was to show the captives in Babylon that Jerusalem was about to fall to the armies of Nebuchadnezzar. False prophets in both Judah and Babylon were declaring that God would never let the holy city fall into the hands of the heathen, but God forewarned His people that it was not the city that was holy but the presence of their God that made the city holy, and they had forsaken their God.

Those who see the glory are not only to speak of it but are to demonstrate it in changed behavior in everyday life. If indeed "the glory of the Lord is risen upon you" (Is. 60:1), then, like Moses, there should be a shine on the face, or, like Ezekiel, there should be a change in our behavior that calls attention to God rather than to ourselves. Ezekiel's whole life became a demonstration of God's presence. So should our lives!

A year and a half later Ezekiel had a third vision of God in His glory, which prepared him to accept the subsequent revelations of the evils and abominations taking place in the temple in Jerusalem by the Jews who had yet to experience Babylonian captivity. He saw seventy of the elders of Israel in darkened rooms of the temple, worshipping idols, while the women were openly weeping not for Jehovah but for Tammuz, a Phoenician deity. Furthermore, he saw "twenty-five men with their backs toward the temple of the Lord and their faces toward the east, and they were worshipping the sun" (Ezek. 8:16). They not only worshipped the heathen gods of the surrounding nations, but they were doing so on the temple site and in the temple itself.

In our generation, the worship of the gods of materialism and humanism is serious enough, but when it is brought into the church—the temple of the living God—it is a double abomination. Paul warned, "Do you not know that you are the temple of God and that the Spirit of God dwells in you? If anyone defiles the temple of God, God will destroy him. For the temple of God is holy, which temple you are" (1 Cor. 3:16,17). Wherever God has chosen to place His glory becomes sacred and holy; whenever we defile that place, God sends judgment upon us and He removes His glory from that place.

The Glory Removed

Because the people had forsaken the "Lord of glory" (James 2:1), the "glory of the Lord went up from the cherub, and paused over the threshold of the temple; and the house was filled with the cloud, and the court was full of the brightness of the Lord's glory" (Ezek. 10:4). When Solomon dedicated this temple, God told him, "If you or your sons at all turn from following Me, and do not keep My commandments and My statutes which I have set before you, but go and serve other gods and worship them, then I will cut off Israel from the land which I have given them; and this house which I have sanctified for My name I will cast out of My sight. Israel will be a proverb and a byword among all peoples" (1 Kings 9:6,7). Forsaking God leads to being forsaken by God—not in the sense of total abandonment, but in the sense of a lost awareness of God's presence.

For several hundred years God's presence had been in the holy of holies of Solomon's temple, and that presence had been its defense, but now, because the people had forsaken the "Lord of glory" (James 2:1), the glory was departing. Soon the temple would be completely destroyed, never again to be rebuilt in such magnificence. How slowly God removed His glory! First He merely shifted it from the holy of holies to the outer court, where for a short season the court was filled with the cloud and brightness of the Lord's glory (see Ezek. 10:4). God had come out from His secret place—that place that was approachable only by the priests—to the humble court of the ordinary people, and for the first time in Ezekiel's writings God's presence is spoken of as a cloud—although it had been visibly demonstrated that way for forty years in the wilderness wanderings.

As if bidding His people good-bye, God's glory remained in the court of the congregation for a short time. Then it ascended above the four cherubim who flew from the city to the Mount of Olives on the east side of the city (see Ezek. 11:23), almost as a prophetic picture of Jesus—God's glory manifest in human form—weeping over Jerusalem. Step by step the symbol of the presence of the Lord left the chosen city. It was as though God forsook them with great reluctance. Perhaps He hoped to be entreated by them not to depart from their midst, so He moved away gradually in order to stir them to plead with Him. But they did not.

If a person's rebellion forces God to withdraw Himself or withhold His gracious influences, He does so with measured and slow steps. God does not hastily leave us to ourselves and our own devices. He waits long to be gracious unto us. He is "the God of patience" (Rom. 15:5), and "He delights in mercy" (Mic. 7:18).

The great nation-wide revivals of history did not die overnight. Long after religion had codified and regulated all responses to God, long after people became aware of personalities and programs rather than the presence of God, the cloud of the divine presence lingered in the land, moving from one group to another in hopes that someone would make room for God's glory to reside among them permanently. No solitary action caused God to depart, nor did He hastily withdraw His presence. A residue of revival lingered in the land for years. But if you could visit, as I have, some of the countries that once brought the knowledge of the glory of God to the world, you would be heartbroken; the glory has departed. Just as "Ichabod"—the glory has departed—became a byword for Israel after her departure from God and God's subsequent departure from her, so "the glory has departed" describes many countries whose people once walked in covenants with God.

Exactly the same thing can be said of individuals who once had the presence of the glory of God in their lives; their hearts have turned to something short of God. For long seasons after their change of heart, God dwells with them. They know hours of His tender presence. Scriptures, sermons and songs tug at their heartstrings. God was reluctant to leave a person in whom He had invested so much, but departure from God forces a departure of God's manifested presence. A person's choice determines God's action, but He withdraws reluctantly and generally in progressive stages.

We live in a highly secularized society in which God has less and less place. Business, politics and science have become autonomous. Religious education, if it has survived at all, is just one subject among many, not the inspiration of all learning and teaching. God does not seem to enter into the deliberations of statesmen;

scientists present a world view that doesn't include God; historians assume that no supernatural actor is involved in the story of our race. Even in the church we often find "religion" rather than God. We lack the vivid sense of His presence or the conviction that He is doing great things and that we have a share in them. Sermons deal with problems that arise from the apparent absence of God rather than with the joyful proclamation of His presence in our midst.

Should we wonder, then, at the withdrawal of God's presence? We have so filled the temple with our base objects of worship that there is no room left for God. If we insist upon calling up the demons of the underworld, we shouldn't be surprised to be torn to pieces by them. God's presence was our defense, but our sins have caused that presence to depart, leaving us defenseless.

I sometimes hear people say that the price of maintaining the presence of God is too high, but this is because they have never weighed the cost of obedience against the terrible price of disobedience. Those who have experienced a protracted season of God's glory in their lives and homes have no basis for understanding the great devastation that will occur when that presence is finally rejected and removed. It is like the homeowner who complained about the high taxes for fire protection until his house was on fire.

The Glory Recompensing

Shortly after Ezekiel saw the glory of God pass to the courtyard of the house, the destroying angels began their work of slaughter in the temple and in the city. The destroyers moved at the command of the Lord of glory. When Ezekiel sought to intercede for his people, the Lord told him, "My eye will neither spare, nor will I have pity, but I will recompense their deeds on their own head" (Ezek. 9:10). Ezekiel watched further as the Lord instructed the man with the inkhorn at his side to "go in among the wheels, under the cherub, fill your hands with coals of fire from among the cherubim, and scatter them over the city" (Ezek. 10:2). History credits the destruction of Jerusalem to the Babylonian army, but God took full responsibility for it when He had coals from the cherubim scattered over the city.

These coals, which had once purged Isaiah from his sin, now dealt with sinners, not with sin. The difference lies in the relationship a person has with God. Those who draw near to God will be purged by the fire of His presence; those who withdraw from Him will be punished by that same coal of fire. God told Ezekiel, "But as for those whose hearts walk after the heart of their detestable things and their abominations, I will recompense their deeds on their own heads" (Ezek. 11:21). Twice, then, God said that His action was to "recompense their deeds." God was getting indemnification, requittal, amends or satisfaction for wrongs committed against Him. It is part of the prophetic message: when men refuse to obey God, they do not escape His rule over them; they only ensure that it functions against them in judgment.

Throughout the Bible, these "burning coals of fire," which were taken from among the cherubim, refer to incandescent wood. David used this same phrase when he wrote, "Then the earth shook and trembled; the foundations of heaven moved and shook, because He was angry. Smoke went up from His nostrils, and devouring

145

fire from His mouth; coals were kindled by it" (2 Sam. 22:8,9; Ps. 18:7,8). Here the vision of Ezekiel, in which the living creatures were incandescent—"bathed in" but not consumed by the fire that played around them— followed in the path of previous symbols: the burning bush (see Ex. 3:2); the pillar of fire by night (see Ex. 13:21,22); the fire on Sinai (see Ex. 19:18); the "fire of the Lord" (see Num. 11:1-3); and the "fire of God" (see 2 Kings 1:12). Quite consistently throughout the Scriptures, fire, as distinct from light, seems to be the symbol of God manifested against evil. As I previously noted, both testaments declare that our "God is a consuming fire" (Deut. 4:24; Heb. 12:29).

The message of grace often blinds our eyes to the truth of divine judgment, but God, who remits our confessed sins, recompenses our continued sins. Ask Adam about the certainty of divine judgment upon rebellion, or look at the thousands of Hebrews who perished in the wilderness for rebellion even after God had so miraculously delivered them from Egyptian bondage. The protective presence of the glory of the Lord is forfeited when we reject God's ways.

When the Lord completely withdrew His manifest presence from the city, the people were at the mercy of their enemies; troubles came on them fast and furiously. So it will be with us. Nothing can impede God; when He forms a purpose, He executes it without the slightest deviation. He has all forms of power at His disposal; He is free and sovereign to do as He wills, and He is unswerving in all that He does. In exacting recompense from the Israelites who had given themselves to idolatry, God chose to use the ungodly king Nebuchadnezzar, whom He called "My servant" (see

Jer. 43:10), for everyone and everything are at God's disposal to do His bidding. What chance has any one of us to withstand Him in the day of His judgment? It is little wonder, then, that the New Testament declares, "For we know Him who said, 'Vengeance is Mine; I will repay, says the Lord.' And again, 'The Lord will judge His people.' It is a fearful thing to fall into the hands of the living God" (Heb. 10:30,31).

In *The Biblical Illustrator*, Joseph Exell adds further insight into the meaning of fire: "As regards the use of fire as a symbol in Holy Scripture, while it is true that it often represents the punitive wrath of God, it is equally certain that it has not always this meaning. Quite as often it is the symbol of God's purifying energy and might. Fire was not the symbol of Jehovah's vengeance in the burning bush. When the Lord is represented as sitting 'as a refiner and purifier of silver,' surely the thought is not of vengeance, but of purifying mercy. We should rather say that fire, in Scripture usage, is the symbol of the intense energy of the divine nature, which continually acts upon every person and on everything, according to the nature of each person or thing; here conserving, there destroying, now cleansing, now consuming" (Hebrews; Volume II).

Fire is a great purifier, and it was used as such in the tabernacle and temple rituals of worship. When fire is used to speak of the nature of God, it tells us that God's nature is so terribly and essentially pure that it cannot help warring against and destroying all that is impure. It defines God's burning love as that which, like fire, assimilates everything to its own perfect purity.

Even as He was removing His presence from His people, God had coals of fire cast among them, purifying them and purging the force that had defiled them. God derives no pleasure from punishing people, but He has committed Himself, by His Word, to present the church "to Himself a glorious church, not having spot or wrinkle or any such thing, but that it should be holy and without blemish" (Eph. 5:27). To accomplish this task, God, as a consuming fire, comes against not only the impurity in the lives of His chosen people, but also against everything that causes that impurity.

If it becomes necessary to destroy a temple in order to keep God's people from going into idolatry, that temple will be torn apart stone by stone. If a sacred place has turned hearts away from God, it will be consumed by fire. Our jealous God comes against the tempter and the temptation with a raging fury that none can withstand. We are not only saved by the power of God, but as Peter, who sinned grievously when he denied the Lord, declared, we "are kept by the power of God" (1 Pet. 1:5). By the fire of His very nature God reveals Himself, refines us and removes from our lives all that would separate us from Himself—even if that means that He must remove His manifested presence from our lives.

The Glory Returned

The glory—the visual manifestation of God's intense energy—was lifted from the Mount of Olives and then disappeared from the prophet's view. The fiery, brilliant demonstration of God's presence—the glory—departed from Israel...but where did it go? God told Ezekiel, "Although I have scattered them among the countries, yet I shall be a little sanctuary for them in the countries where they have gone" (Ezek. 11:16). Notice God's words: a "little sanctuary"—a little "dwelling place." God drove His people out of their land, destroyed their holy city and its temple, and then followed them into exile and became a sanctuary to them.

The rabbis chose to speak of God's manifested presence on the earth as the *shekinah*. This is not a biblical word, but it is consistently used in the Jewish Targums—rabbinical commentaries on the Old Testament—to designate "the divine presence" or "the divine manifestation." The word is used exclusively of God, and it refers not to the fire, cloud or rainbow manifestations but to Jehovah, who caused the manifestation. The word itself comes from a Hebrew root, *sh-k-n*, meaning "that which dwells or resides"; hence *shekinah*, which means "to dwell." The rabbis used this word to avoid any localization of God. They consistently conceived of God as being omnipresent, but they fully recognized a sense in which God revealed His presence among His people, and they referred to this as the *shekinah*.

Scholars tell us that bilingual Jews substituted the Greek word for "tabernacle" for the Hebrew word *shekinah* (the two words were similar in sound and meaning). When the apostle John said, "The Word became flesh and dwelt among us" (John 1:14), the early Hebrew Christians mentally replaced the word "dwelt" with *shekinah*. God *shekinahed*, or "tabernacled," among us. Similarly, they understood John's declaration "Behold, the tabernacle of God is with men, and He will dwell with them, and they shall be His people, and God Himself will be with them and be their God" (Rev. 21:3) to mean "the *shekinah* of God is with men, and He will *shekinah* (tabernacle) with them."

The actual equivalent of the Hebrew word *shekinah* is the Greek word *doxa*, or "glory." In several instances *doxa* refers to God or a manifestation-form of God. In describing the tabernacle in the wilderness, the New Testament says, "Above it were the cherubim of glory (*doxa*) overshadowing the mercy seat" (Heb. 9:5); Paul, speaking of the Israelites, stated, "To whom pertain the adoption, the glory (*doxa*), the covenants, the giving of the law, the service of God, and the promises" (Rom. 9:4). He was obviously referring to the *shekinah*, or manifest demonstration of God in the midst of Israel.

In the closing chapters of Ezekiel's book there is a rather detailed description of a magnificent temple, the likes of which have never been constructed in the history of Israel. There is no way it could refer to the small temple that the exiles constructed when they returned and rebuilt Jerusalem, nor is it likely that it refers to some future temple to be erected on the temple site in Jerusalem. It is more probable that Ezekiel was given a figurative glimpse into the glorious New Testament temple called the church (see 1 Cor. 3:16). Just as Ezekiel saw the glory of the Lord depart from the temple in Jerusalem, he saw the *shekinah* return to this magnificent temple in three stages. First, he saw that "the glory of the God of Israel came from the way of the east"; then "the glory of the Lord came into the temple by way of the gate which faces toward the east"; and finally "the glory of the Lord filled the temple" (Ezek. 43:2,4,5).

It was the belief of the Jews that the glory of the Lord did not dwell in the most holy place in the second temple built when the exiles returned to Jerusalem. In the Targums, paraphrases of Jewish Scriptures in Aramaic, Yoma 1 mentioned the *shekinah* in a list of things absent from the reconstructed temple. If the visible glory of God's manifest presence left the land of Israel to tabernacle temporarily among the exiles, if God's glory eventually returned to the temple Ezekiel envisioned but did not appear in the temple that the Jews constructed, where has that glory returned?

In the minds of the Jewish teachers a new direction of thought came to stay, and the glory slowly became eschatological, so that in the New Testament we find it is an integral part of the life of the kingdom of God—in the present and in the future. The actual and the eschatological elements dynamically come together in the person of Jesus Christ. Our God dwells in light unapproachable (see 1 Tim. 6:16), and his *doxa* (glory) shone about the shepherds when Christ's birth was announced; it was made known in Christ, and through Him men apprehended the presence of God. Even after death Jesus was "glorified" and sat down at the right hand of God. From that moment on, visions of Christ have come in the same form as the visions of God: brightness and light (see Acts 22:6,7). In the New Testament the glory of Christ is identifiable with the glory of God, and God's glory is revealed "in the face of Jesus Christ" (2 Cor. 4:6).

Throughout the New Testament, Christ is the glory of God made visible to those whose eyes are opened to see it. John defined it positively when he wrote, "We beheld His glory (*doxa*), the glory as of the only begotten of the Father, full of grace and truth" (John 1:14). The whole human life of Christ was a continuous and conscious manifestation of divine glory, but that glory, like the Old Testament *shekinah,* was largely veiled from view. God's glory had once been in a cloud and fire, but when Jesus was in human form, God's glory was hidden in the incarnation. It flashed out in miracles and words of wisdom, but largely there was "no beauty that we should desire Him" (Is. 53:2). The glory was there, but the prince of the darkness of this world so blinded people that they saw only His humanity and not God's *shekinah* manifestation. His glory became fully apparent only at the transfiguration, for there the cloud, the symbol of the divine presence, came over the disciples and Jesus, and His exceedingly great glory was seen in His countenance and even in His garments (see Matt. 17:2).

The Glory Remaining

The glory has returned both to Israel and—resplendently—to the church, but that glory shall be displayed even more in days to come. Isaiah declared, "They shall see the glory of the Lord, the excellency of our God" (Is. 35:2) and "the glory of the Lord shall be revealed, and all flesh shall see it together; for the mouth of the Lord has spoken" (Is. 40:5). Perhaps this has not yet happened nationally, but it most certainly is happening individually. Just as God's glory left the temple and became "a little sanctuary" among the captives in Babylon, so the *shekinah* of God that has been rejected in much of organized religion has tabernacled with individual believers, transforming their lives "from glory to glory, just as by the Spirit of the Lord" (2 Cor. 3:18). But God revealed to Habakkuk that "the earth will be filled with the knowledge of the glory of the Lord, as the waters cover the sea" (Hab. 2:14). What was once a corporate revelation became an individual experience, but it shall someday be worldwide knowledge. *Immanuel*—"God with us"—will become so real that "all flesh shall see it together."

Just how God will accomplish this is in His planning

and power, but the future of the Christian may well be considered as the restoration of the *doxa* lost at the fall. Adam must have been radiant with God's glory. Actually, tradition declares that Adam and Eve were clothed with that glory. Adam lost that glory, but God purposes to restore it to humanity. David, under the inspiration of the *shekinah*, sang, "What is man that You are mindful of him?...You have crowned him with glory and honor" (Ps. 8:4,5). Under present conditions this is realized only in Christ, for Christ is the true image of God (see 2 Cor. 4:4), and we are even now "being transformed into the same image from glory to glory" (2 Cor. 3:18), so that it is "Christ in you, the hope of glory" (Col. 1:27). Ultimately, redeemed persons shall be conformed to Christ's image, for we are "predestined to be conformed to the image of His Son" (Rom. 8:29), and "we shall be like Him, for we shall see Him as He is" (1 John 3:2).

With the glory restored to them, Christians will become what they were originally intended to be: lovers and worshippers of God. Like Adam, who walked daily with the Lord, we "also will appear with Him in glory" (Col. 3:4).

Ezekiel's first response to his initial vision was to prostrate himself in the dust of the earth before the majestic splendor of God's glory (see Ezek. 1:28), for worship is a natural response to an awareness of God's presence. Ezekiel had not even seen the glory of the Lord—only "the *appearance of the likeness* of the glory of the Lord"—but he was overpowered by the dazzling luster of what he saw. He immediately prostrated himself in a humble sense of his own unworthiness and of the infinite distance he perceived to be between himself and God, and he worshipped "the God of glory."

The more of Himself God makes known to us, the more we should bow ourselves in humble submission to Him, and the more we should adore His majesty and open our spiritual minds to hear His voice. This is the response of the saints of ages past, and this will be the eternal response of saints in the ages to come, for we read, "And all the angels stood around the throne and the elders and the four living creatures, and fell on their faces before the throne and worshipped God, saying: 'Amen! Blessing and glory and wisdom, thanksgiving and honor and power and might, be to our God forever and ever. Amen' " (Rev. 7:11,12).

The final words given to Ezekiel are *YHWH Shammah*, which are translated "The Lord is there" (Ezek. 48:35). Ezekiel was promised an abiding, a remaining, of God's presence. God is present whether or not we see the lightning, hear the voices or feel the heat of the flames. It is not the cherubim's cry, "Blessed is the glory of the Lord from His place!" (Ezek. 3:12), that produces God's *shekinah*. That proclamation is only a response to it; but if that is the high-level angelic response, what should be the earthly response of redeemed men and women?

God revealed Himself to Ezekiel not by propositions regarding His character but in a personal encounter. Ancient rabbis insisted that no one under the age of thirty read this part of Ezekiel's book. Why? Because they were conscious that here they were standing on holy ground. So was Ezekiel, who like Simon Peter when confronted by the supernatural ability of Jesus (see Luke 5:8) could only fall on his face as one dead. In every generation it is the true prophet's hallmark. The false prophet can chatter glibly about God because he has never met Him, but the prophet of God comes out from the divine presence indelibly marked with the glory of his Lord. Our only adequate response to such a God is awed worship and obedient devotion.

It would be good for us to recover something of that awe in the presence of God. The shallowness of our generation's concepts of God is reflected in the superficial songs and utterances we often call "worship" and in the lack of deep reverential feelings for God. Perhaps we are like Job, who confessed to God, "I have heard of You by the hearing of the ear, but now my eye sees You. Therefore I abhor myself, and repent in dust and ashes" (Job 42:5,6).

God is "the God of glory," and He cannot be God without His glory. The intention of God is that mankind and all creation should give glory to Him and show forth His excellencies. This is well summed up in the Westminster Shorter Catechism: "Man's chief end is to glorify God." Paul recognized this when he wrote, "Now to the King eternal, immortal, invisible, to God who alone is wise, be honor and glory forever and ever. Amen" (1 Tim. 1:17).

God's unchanging purpose, as repeatedly spoken through Ezekiel, remains "that you may know that I am God." Ezekiel met the God of glory, but Daniel met this "God who alone is wise," for God continued to reveal Himself in broader and broader concepts as He persisted in bringing mankind back to the revelation of Himself that Adam once possessed but forfeited through sin.

chapter eight

DANIEL MET A REVEALING GOD

"...God has revealed them to us...."
(1 Corinthians 2:10)

Ezekiel ended his book with the compound name of God *Jehovah-Shammah*, "the Lord is there," suggesting that the *shekinah* of God's presence had moved from Israel to Babylon to be with His people. The two great miracles recorded in the Book of Daniel proved that God was as close to His people in Babylon as He had been in Jerusalem or in the temple. He walked in the fiery furnace with Hananiah, Mishael and Azariah, and He spent the night with Daniel in the lions' den. All four were divinely preserved as a witness to both the Gentile kings and the Hebrew people that, captors or captives, *Shammah*—God was there! Ezekiel sought to reveal God's purpose and presence to the Israelites in their captivity, while Daniel was chosen by God to reveal God's purposes and presence to the Gentiles who were the captors.

Although the Babylonian captivity was severe, it was

far less a punishment than a cure for the Hebrews. Because they had persisted in idolatry, God had placed them in a land noted for the multitude of its idols, very much as their ancestors had been in a land of idols in Egypt. Just as a display of power over Egypt's idols had made believers of that generation, so God, by a repeated display of supernatural wisdom and divine power, showed His superiority over the Babylonian idols in order that His people, as well as these Gentiles, might see the contrast and choose to serve the true God.

Daniel's Hebrew name means "God is judge or prince," while the Babylonian name given to him, Belteshazzar, means "Bel's prince." Born to the royal family, probably as one of King Hezekiah's descendants, he and three other intelligent, well-educated Hebrew youths were taken in their late teens in the first deportation from Israel in 605 B.C. They were assigned to serve in King Nebuchadnezzar's court. The king changed their residence, their names, their occupation, their language and their food, but Nebuchadnezzar could never change their character. The reputation of Daniel was so great that even in his lifetime it became a proverb. When writing to the king of Tyre, Ezekiel ironically said, "Behold, you are wiser than Daniel!" (Ezek. 28:3), and in writing about the impending destruction of Jerusalem he said, "Though these three men, Noah, Daniel, and Job, were in it, they would deliver only themselves by their righteousness...they would deliver neither sons nor daughters, but only they themselves..." (Ezek. 14:14,18,20).

Daniel is one of the few people of whom the Scriptures speak only good, and he seemed to have had a place in God's heart much as John did in the days of

Jesus, for three times Daniel is called "greatly beloved" (see Dan. 9:23; 10:11,19).

Daniel's book is basically a history book, and in the Jewish canon of Scripture it is placed in "the writings" rather than among the prophets. Some of the history is written in first person prose, while much of it is given in apocalyptic visions of the future and is written in symbols, very much like the New Testament book of Revelation.

Daniel, the government servant and statesman, did not fit the Hebrew concept of a prophet, for the Hebrew prophet had a special function to fulfill under the theocracy. His special task was to be the authorized teacher of the people. He was essentially the preacher of righteousness to his generation, and it was only incidentally that he predicted the future. But Daniel was almost exactly the opposite of this pattern. He came on the scene not as a preacher but as one who revealed the secrets of God concerning coming world governments. His writing is far more revelatory than predictive. It does not evidence the style of Job or Solomon which, typical of Hebrew wisdom, involved the solving of riddles and perplexing questions. Instead, Daniel presented the future in a series of unfolding pictures, using symbols that are an enigma to most of us except where they are divinely explained.

Back in the early 1700s, Matthew Henry wrote: "Daniel, indeed, appears far more glorious as the prophet of Jehovah, than as the prime minister of the medes and persians. He was admitted to converse with angels, nay, with the Lord of angels, and was declared by him to be 'a man greatly beloved.' In answer to his prayer, the various revolutions to take place in the empires of the world, and the rebuilding of Jerusalem, were made known to him. He received the clearest information respecting the person, the office, the work, and the benefit of the great Redeemer; the precise time of his appearance, the nature and design of his sufferings; also the troubles and persecutions of the church, the conversion of the jewish nation, the resurrection of the dead, and the final consummation of all things'' (Matthew Henry and Thomas Scott, *Commentary on the Holy Bible*, Volume 2, page 364).

Josephus, the Jewish historian, speaks of Daniel as one of the greatest of the prophets, whose writings were in daily use among the Jews. He observes that Daniel differs widely from all other prophets, who fundamentally foretold disastrous events, while Daniel predicted the most joyous events. This writer pictures Daniel as one who wrote under the dictates of an infallible Spirit, who not only predicted events but declared the time of their fulfillment (see Josephus, Anti. lib. x., c. 12).

Adam Clarke wrote, ''We cannot help thinking that God had given this eminent man a greater degree of light to fix the times when his predictions should issue, than he had given in general to all his predecessors, who simply declared the mind of God in relation to things *future* without attempting to indicate the *distance of time* in which they should be fulfilled. There are but very few exceptions to this either in *Isaiah* or *Jeremiah* (*Clarke's Commentary*, Volume 14, page 558).

Daniel may not have fit the Jew's concept of a prophet, but the prophetic mantle rested beautifully upon him even though it appeared that his office was political rather than prophetic. God delights in choosing the unusual and what appears to be the unfit so that He might be seen supreme within that vessel. In His sovereignty God chooses whom He wills. Daniel was chosen.

Daniel's Key Was God's Omniscience

God would not be a perfect God if He were not complete in knowledge and wisdom. Paul ended his letter to the church at Rome by saying, "...to God, alone wise, be glory..." (Rom. 16:27). Wisdom is characteristic of God, and this wisdom is based upon His complete knowledge of all things. The theological term "omniscience" means that God knows all things within Himself, in the universe and in all creatures. There is nothing that He does not know and has not known from eternity. His knowledge is absolute and unacquired, and He never has to learn anything.

Human knowledge is acquired and unfortunately is more easily forgotten than gained. God does not acquire His knowledge; He has always possessed it. Acquisition of knowledge presupposes ignorance to begin with and implies a limited perspective which is gradually enlarged by effort, and it also assumes dependence upon intermediate sources of knowledge such as books, teachers, evidence and experiment. None of this is applicable to God. He could never have been ignorant, and He has never been dependent upon anything or any person external to Himself for obtaining information.

Knowledge, however important, is but a part of our human lives. It is conceivable that mankind could be without knowledge and still have life, but knowledge is not a separable entity in God. God does not possess knowledge and wisdom; He *is* omniscient. In Him there can be no progression from a lower to a higher plane of knowledge, much less from ignorance to knowledge. Inherent in God are all the treasures of wisdom and

MEETING GOD

knowledge which have always been exactly what they
now are. As St. Augustine said, for God "to know is
the same thing as to exist."

In addition to perfect knowledge, omniscience in-
volves perfect understanding and perfect wisdom. God
not only possesses all the facts, but He has full perception and interpretation of those facts, and He exhibits
perfect wisdom in the application of what He knows.

The Bible does not use the word "omniscience," but
it does demonstrate omniscience in speaking of the
foreknowledge of God (Rom. 8:29), of God's foresee-
ing (Gal. 3:8), of His foretelling (through prophecy—
Acts 3:18-24), and of His foreordinations (1 Peter 1:20).
Actually, the truth of God's omniscience is seen from
Genesis to Revelation. The Book of Job, the oldest book
in the Bible, speaks of the "wondrous works of Him
who is perfect in knowledge" (Job 37:16); the psalmist
sang, "His understanding is infinite" (Ps. 147:5); the
prophet cried, "There is no searching of His understanding" (Is. 40:28); the apostle John declared, "God...
knows all things" (1 John 3:20). God says of Himself,
"I am God, and there is none like Me, declaring the
end from the beginning, and from ancient times things
that are not yet done, saying, 'My counsel shall stand,
and I will do all My pleasure' " (Is. 46:9,10). "Oh,
the depth of the riches both of the wisdom and
knowledge of God! How unsearchable are His
judgments and His ways past finding out!" (Rom.
11:33).

God knows the world in its totality. This knowledge
extends from the minute to the magnificent, and it
simultaneously covers all the divisions of time—the past,
present and future alike. No human can ever give God

"unknown" information, for God, who is everywhere present concurrently, knows all things seen and unseen, spoken and unspoken, both human and divine.

David came to grips with this reality in one of his psalms to the chief musician, in which he sang, "O Lord, You have searched me and known me. You know my sitting down and my rising up; You understand my thought afar off. You comprehend my path and my lying down, and are acquainted with all my ways. For there is not a word on my tongue, but behold, O Lord, You know it altogether. You have hedged me behind and before, and laid Your hand upon me. Such knowledge is too wonderful for me; it is high, I cannot attain it" (Ps. 139:1-6).

God Revealed His Omniscience

The omniscience of God is never questioned by Bible authors. It was expected that the ever-present, invisible, almighty Jehovah possessed infinite knowledge. Nor was God's ability to communicate with His creatures held in dispute, for God had been speaking to mankind from Adam's time on. The uniqueness of the Book of Daniel lies neither in its amazing apocalyptic knowledge nor in God's communication of that knowledge; the fact that the information concerned the Gentiles rather than the Jews is what sets this book apart from others. Other prophets had spoken of God's judgment upon Gentile nations, but Daniel revealed that, by God's design, Gentiles, not Jews, were to have political power and supremacy in the world.

God gloriously demonstrated His power to the Babylonians, and in addition to that He sent Daniel to the courts of the Babylonian kings to represent Him there and to teach the Gentile monarchs His sovereign will concerning all nations of the world. It is made obvious here that Gentile as well as Jew must learn that continuance of power and blessing is dependent upon rendering worship and obedience to God. Repeatedly it was the omniscience of God, revealed through Daniel as divine wisdom, that opened the kings to receive instruction and warning from God. God did not empower and then abandon them; He chose them and then sought to guide them. Daniel was positioned by God for this specific task, and he was given a series of revelations that enabled him to know what the king saw or what God had enabled Daniel himself to see.

The Message of the Revelations

Many books have been written about the meaning of Daniel's apocalyptic visions, and there is diversity of opinion on some of it. It is not my purpose to attempt an exegetical study of Daniel in a short chapter, but sometimes in looking at details we overlook the larger picture. Without seeking to interpret symbols or even individual revelations, we can be both blessed and benefited in looking at the fundamental message of this book. At the risk of oversimplification, let me suggest five basic messages in the Book of Daniel.

The first is that the age of the Gentiles was provided by God. Nebuchadnezzar's dream of the great image (chapter 2) establishes this. God had offered world supremacy to the Jews (see Deut. 28) on the condition of obedience to Him, but the Jews did not comply with that condition. So, beginning about 600 B.C., God withdrew the offer and gave the supremacy to the Gentiles, starting with the nation of Babylon. Nebuchadnezzar, as absolute monarch of Babylon, was made master of the world and was given an opportunity: He could continue in power on the same condition of obedience to God that the Jews had received and rejected.

In Nebuchadnezzar's vision of the great and awesome image, God let both Jew and Gentile know that world dominion would be held by the Gentiles for a lengthy season. The Jews, who hoped for a short captivity and then complete restoration, were to learn that world government would be in the hands of the Gentiles for a very protracted season, and the Gentiles, who were granted leadership by divine permission, needed to know that it was not their strength or cleverness that had given them the dominion. The very fact that they were envisioned first as gold and then as clay indicated depreciation, not appreciation.

A second message was companion to the first. Nebuchadnezzar's second dream, where he saw himself as a giant tree cut down and then reduced to the level of an animal, contained the message "that the Most High rules in the kingdom of men, gives it to whomever He will, and sets over it the lowest of men" (Dan. 4:17). Nebuchadnezzar sought to be more than a man, but God righteously made him less than a man. God raises up and puts down whom He wills, and He wanted these early Gentile kings to know this.

The third message is found in the fulfillment of that dream. One year after Daniel interpreted the dream, the king was walking in the royal palace and said, " 'Is not this great Babylon, that I have built for a royal dwelling by my mighty power and for the honor of my majesty?' While the word was still in the king's mouth, a voice fell from heaven: 'King Nebuchadnezzar, to you it is spoken: the kingdom has departed from you!' " (Dan. 4:30,31). God wanted these Gentile monarchs to know that pride—which puts us instead of God on the throne—brings God's punishment to Jew and Gentile alike. Nothing will move a person from God's position of exaltation faster than personal pride.

A fourth message unfolded at Belshazzar's feast when the finger of God wrote a coded message on the wall (chapter 5). God clearly indicated that all authority and power comes from Him and that all worship must be given to the omniscient One. Sinners are pleased with gods that neither see nor know, but they will be judged by One to whom all things are open. Nothing we do, say or even think escapes the awareness of Him with whom we have to do, for "the eyes of the Lord are in every place, keeping watch on the evil and the good" (Prov. 15:3). God's knowledge is perfect. He never errs, changes or overlooks anything.

In the privacy of the banquet hall the king used golden cups from Jehovah's temple to toast his heathen gods, but he quickly learned that "there is no creature hidden from His sight, but all things are naked and open to the eyes of Him to whom we must give account" (Heb. 4:13). Accordingly, God numbered Belshazzar's kingdom, finished it, divided it and gave it to the Medes and Persians, and this powerful king found himself powerless to prevent it.

The fifth message summarized the preceding four: God reigns, and His kingdom is an everlasting kingdom. After his restoration, Nebuchadnezzar "blessed the Most High and praised and honored Him who lives forever: for His dominion is an everlasting dominion, and His kingdom is from generation to generation" (Dan. 4:34). Many years later, after the incident of the lions' den, King Darius, the Mede, said of God, "He is the living God, and steadfast forever; His kingdom is the one which shall not be destroyed, and His dominion shall endure to the end'' (Dan. 6:26).

In the vision of the four beasts, Daniel wrote, ''I watched till thrones were put in place, and the Ancient of Days was seated; His garment was white as snow, and the hair of His head was like pure wool. His throne was a fiery flame, its wheels a burning fire; a fiery stream issued and came forth from before Him, a thousand thousands ministered to Him; ten thousand times ten thousand stood before Him. The court was seated, and the books were opened...and behold, One like the Son of Man, coming with the clouds of heaven! He came to the Ancient of Days, and they brought Him near before Him. Then to Him was given dominion and glory and a kingdom, that all peoples, nations, and languages should serve Him. His dominion is an everlasting dominion, which shall not pass away, and His kingdom the one which shall not be destroyed'' (Dan. 7:9,10,13,14).

What God taught the Gentile kings through the revelations given to Daniel needs to be learned in the church today. The age of the church has been ordained by God as surely as the times of the Gentiles have been God's ordination. Because God raises up and puts down whom He wills in the church, power politics are totally unnecessary and unfruitful. It may gain authority over men, but authority given by God cannot be gained through a ballot box.

Perhaps we Christians need to be reminded that all authority and power come from God. Jesus said so, and that settles it. We have no might beyond the power God has conferred upon us, and anything that is conferred can be removed. In light of this, we need to guard against pride—as if we have achieved position or power through our own abilities. Just as surely as pride brings God's punishment to earthly rulers, it equally brings God's punishment upon members of Christ's ruling authority on earth today: the church.

In the midst of all the confusion and conflict in the various branches of the visible church on earth, it is refreshing to remember that God reigns and that His kingdom is an everlasting kingdom. Long after the religious kingdom-builders of our generation have been laid in their graves, God's kingdom will still be increasing here on the earth.

The Manner of the Revelations

The manifold revelations that Daniel received came to him in a variety of ways. We are comfortable with sameness, but God delights in variety and in preventing us from making a ritual out of a relationship with Him. When Nebuchadnezzar had his first dream and threatened to kill all the wise men of his realm because no one could explain the meaning of the dream to him, Daniel gathered his three Hebrew friends together and informed them of the situation "that they might seek mercies from the God of heaven concerning this secret, so that Daniel and his companions might not perish with the rest of the wise men of Babylon. Then the secret was revealed to Daniel in a night vision" (Dan. 2:18,19). Four praying men touched the heart of God, who graciously revealed a measure of His omniscience to Daniel in a vision.

Has God changed in this twentieth century? We are assured, "If any of you lacks wisdom, let him ask of God, who gives to all liberally and without reproach, and it will be given to him" (James 1:5). One of the great by-products of time spent in communion with God is the impartation of divine information and wisdom that comes by hearing God's voice. On repeated occasions Daniel had seasons of prayer and received a measure of the mind of God.

Daniel received not only the interpretation of dreams, but he sometimes received communication from God in dreams, for we read, "Daniel had a dream and visions of his head while on his bed" (Dan. 7:1). Sometimes God is able to communicate best with us when our conscious minds cannot interfere with the impressions God is giving. Jacob had his first confrontation with God in a dream, and Joseph was given foresight into his future in three dreams. In Bible times God repeatedly used dreams as a channel of communication, and God declares, "I am the Lord, I do not change" (Mal. 3:6). Perhaps if our minds were more centered on God when we went to bed, we might be more qualified to hear from God in our sleep.

A third manner of communicating with Daniel was by the written Word of God, as is evidenced in the handwriting on the wall during Belshazzar's feast. Daniel gave far more than a literal interpretation of the three words; God gave Daniel an illumination of the full message, and he in turn gave it to the king.

One of the safest avenues of communication from God is His written Word—the Bible. In it are hidden the rich treasures of the knowledge of God, which, when illuminated by the Holy Spirit, instruct, guide, inspire and guard our daily lives. It is amazing what a serious reader of God's Word will learn about God, about self and about the environment.

Still another avenue for revelation was books, for

when Daniel "understood by the books the number of the years specified by the word of the Lord, given through Jeremiah the prophet, that He would accomplish seventy years in the desolations of Jerusalem" (Dan. 9:2), he began intercession by prayer and supplications, with fasting, sackcloth and ashes—seeking the restoration of God's people to the promised land. He entered into a prior revelation of truth with fresh understanding. God illuminated Daniel's mind as he read what God had spoken to Jeremiah. Of course, to us Jeremiah is part of the Bible. But in Daniel's day it had not yet been accepted into the scriptural canon; it was but a book. Often God speaks a measure of truth to a person, and because that truth is written in book form, it becomes available to a multitude of hungry people. How often God has spoken to my heart while I was reading the writings of others. None of us has the full truth—God has divided it among many—so we need to hear what has been revealed to other members of the body of Christ.

On several occasions Daniel was given revelation by an angel of the Lord, or perhaps it was *the* angel of the Lord. On at least two occasions the angel's name is given as Gabriel. Repeatedly throughout the Old Testament, God sent angels as messengers to earth. Stephen, the first martyr of the Christian church, declared that even the law was given through the mediacy of angels (see Acts 7:53).

In speaking of angels, the writer of Hebrews asked, "Are they not all ministering spirits sent forth to minister for those who will inherit salvation?" (Heb. 1:14). Since angels are usually anonymous messengers, we are probably unaware of the many times angels have ministered to us, but throughout the Bible they were active in the affairs of God's chosen people, and the church is God's chosen people in the New Testament era. Revelation by angelic messenger is as possible today as it was in Daniel's time. If that is what it takes to get the revelation through to us, that is what God will use.

The most common method God used to communicate with Daniel was by vision. (The word "vision" appears twenty-two times, and ten more times in the plural form.) The use of vision in the Old Testament seems consistent with the manifest nature of God, for throughout the Scriptures God is declared as revealing Himself and making His ways known to chosen people through visions. "Hear now My words: If there is a prophet among you, I, the Lord, make Myself known to him in a vision, and I speak to him in a dream" (Num. 12:6).

Biblical use of the word "vision" places the emphasis on dimensions seen by other-than-ordinary sight— something beheld as in a dream or ecstasy, an image without corporeal presence. When the New Testament loosely quotes from Isaiah 64:4, "Eye has not seen, nor ear heard, nor have entered into the heart of man the things which God has prepared for those who love Him," it adds, "But God has revealed them to us through His Spirit. For the Spirit searches all things, yes, the deep things of God" (1 Cor. 2:9, 10). The New Testament does not limit revelation by vision to prophets. As a matter of fact, the first two gifts of the Spirit, which operate in believers without the necessity of an office, are "the word of wisdom" and "the word of knowledge" (1 Cor. 12:8). The indwelling Spirit gives an insight, an illumination, an understanding of the mind and will of God, and shares it with believers a word at a time.

The Means of the Revelations

For God to reveal something to Daniel was one thing, but to reveal the same thing successfully to a heathen king required attention-getting tactics, and God is, of course, a master at getting our attention. He used four principal means to communicate through Daniel to the monarchs of the Babylonians, the Medes and the Persians: dreams, demonstrations, divulgences and declarations. In each of these, Daniel and his companions proved to be the key to unlocking God's message to Gentile kings.

Twice God gave King Nebuchadnezzar disturbing dreams, and both times Jehovah gave Daniel the correct interpretation for the dreams. The first dream told the king of his greatness in God's plan for Gentile world leadership, and the second told him that because of his pride and self-exaltation, God was going to cut him down and remove him from being king of Babylon. Nebuchadnezzar's response both times was high praise and worship of Jehovah. The first time he praised Daniel's God (see Dan. 2:47), but the second time he proclaimed, "Now I, Nebuchadnezzar, praise and extol and honor the King of heaven, all of whose works are truth, and His ways justice. And those who walk in pride He is able to abase" (Dan. 4:37). Message received!

Another means that God used to reveal Himself to Gentile kings was demonstration of His power to deliver those who served Him. First there was the fiery furnace for Shadrach, Meshach and Abed-Nego (the Babylonian names for the three Hebrew children). What a demonstration this was to the king and all of his kingdom, including the Hebrew captives who needed to be delivered from idolatry. Many years and three kings later, God used a second demonstration of divine power when Darius, the Mede, was tricked into having Daniel thrown into the lions' den. When the king found Daniel alive and well, he wrote, "To all peoples, nations, and languages that dwell in all the earth: Peace be multiplied to you. I make a decree that in every dominion of my kingdom men must tremble and fear before the God of Daniel. For He is the living God, and steadfast forever; His kingdom is the one which shall not be destroyed, and His dominion shall endure to the end. He delivers and rescues, and He works signs and wonders in heaven and on earth, who has delivered Daniel from the power of the lions" (Dan. 6:25-27). Again, message received and understood!

The prime example of God revealing His sovereignty and omniscience through divulgence was in giving the meaning of the handwriting on the wall when Belshazzar desecrated the sacred vessels of the Lord during a state feast. When the hand of God wrote four words on the wall, "the king's countenance changed, and his thoughts troubled him, so that the joints of his hips were loosened and his knees knocked against each other" (Dan. 5:6). When his learned scholars were unable to read the message, the queen told Belshazzar, "There is a man in your kingdom in whom is the Spirit of the Holy God. And in the days of your father, light and understanding and wisdom, like the wisdom of the gods, were found in him" (Dan. 5:11).

Daniel was called in. He far more than translated the words; he interpreted God's message contained in them.

Belshazzar had failed to learn the lessons taught to his father, Nebuchadnezzar, and therefore God was taking the kingdom from Belshazzar and giving it to Darius that very night. The message was heard and fulfilled: before sunrise Belshazzar was dead; the Babylonian kingdom was captured; the Gentile dominion was transferred to Darius, king of the Medes and Persians. God said it, and God did it!

To the dreams, demonstrations and divulgences Daniel also added God's declarations, for he actually preached righteousness to these Gentile kings with the same fearlessness that prophets had demonstrated in preaching to kings of Judah and Israel. Daniel was convinced that since these kings were in power by God's appointment, they were responsible to live righteously as covenant people.

Whether involved with dreams, demonstrations, divulgences or declarations, Daniel ascribed all the power and glory to God, just as Joseph had before Pharaoh of Egypt. Each proclaimed the great truth that God is not only the source of true knowledge but is the only source of knowledge of the future. In Daniel's aging years God gave him revelations regarding the development of the world power and of God's kingdom—revelations which in their precision excel all other scriptural predictions of the prophets.

Some of the Old Testament prophets seemed to have heard from God once or twice, but Daniel had revelations from God through most of the ninety or more years of his lifetime. They began in the second year of the reign of Nebuchadnezzar and continued until the return of the exiles under Ezra. He received and shared revelations through two world governments and four kings, and his apocalyptic visions revealed events from the days of Nebuchadnezzar to those beyond our present day. Through the revelation of the secrets hidden from the wise men of this world, God proved Himself to Daniel as the God of the fathers, as the true God in opposition to the gods of the heathen.

God Is Inherently a Self-Revealing God

Daniel's paean of praise after receiving his first divine revelation extols God's knowledge and wisdom and God's willingness to share that wisdom with Daniel. He wrote, "Blessed be the name of God forever and ever, for wisdom and might are His. And He changes the times and the seasons; He removes kings and raises up kings; He gives wisdom to the wise and knowledge to those who have understanding. He reveals deep and secret things; He knows what is in the darkness, and light dwells with Him. I thank You and praise You, O God of my fathers; You have given me wisdom and might, and have now made known to me what we asked of You..." (Dan. 2:20-23). Daniel saw God's wisdom as all-embracing and unlimited, but the emphasis throughout his psalm is on the fact that God makes His wisdom available: "He gives wisdom...and knowledge...He reveals....You have given me wisdom and might....You have made known to me...."

In his book titled *The Book of Daniel*, W.C. Stevens commented, "Only to those who are in communion with God belongs the gift of finding from the Most High His hidden purposes and the interpretation of the portentous signs which He holds out to earthly view." But that gift does belong to those who are in communion with God, for Paul prayed "that the God of our Lord Jesus Christ, the Father of glory, may give to you the spirit of wisdom and revelation in the knowledge of Him, the eyes of your understanding being enlightened; that you may know what is the hope of His calling, what are the riches of the glory of His inheritance in the saints, and what is the exceeding greatness of His power toward us who believe..." (Eph. 1:17-19).

We need to remember that the wisdom of God is not separate from God; it is not something He has acquired. Wisdom and God are inseparable. Therefore the New Testament dares to say, "You are in Christ Jesus, who became for us wisdom from God..." (1 Cor. 1:30). As Matthew Henry said, "If we would know the mind of God, we must apply to Christ, in whom are hid all the treasures of wisdom and knowledge; not hid *from* us, but hid *for* us." The availability of Christ to the individual believer, through the indwelling Spirit of God, makes the wisdom and knowledge of God an appropriable reality through faith. That this is based on neither merit nor ability is proved in the Ephesian letter, which states that it is "...according to the riches of His grace which He made to abound toward us in all wisdom and prudence, having made known to us the mystery of His will, according to His good pleasure which He purposed in Himself" (Eph. 1:7-9). God's wisdom is made available to us because of His grace, His pleasure and His purposes, and since these are limitless, we might expect that revelations from God are equally without limit.

Divine Revelation Aids Worship

Recognition of God's infinite knowledge should fill our hearts with adoration for Him. From the beginning, our lives have been open to His view. He foresaw our every fall, our every sin, our every backsliding; yet He fixed His divine love upon us. Oh, how the realization of this should cause us to bow in wonder and worship before Him.

Throughout the Book of Daniel, each revelation, no matter how it came, evoked a praise response from those involved. Daniel consistently gave God all the glory for revelation, but so did the heathen kings. Nebuchadnezzar first responded to God as Daniel's God in saying, "Truly your God is the God of gods, the Lord of kings, and a revealer of secrets, since you could reveal this secret" (Dan. 2:47). After the fiery furnace demonstration he enlarged his concept to envision God as the God of the three Hebrew children as well, for he wrote, "Therefore I make a decree that any people, nation, or language which speaks anything amiss against the God of Shadrach, Meshach, and Abed-Nego shall be cut in pieces, and their houses shall be made an ash heap; because there is no other God who can deliver like this" (Dan. 3:29).

Finally, after God restored Nebuchadnezzar's sanity, he responded to God as his God in reporting, "I blessed the Most High and praised and honored Him who lives forever" (Dan. 4:34), and following this testimony he wrote a beautiful poem extolling the eternity of God's dominion and kingdom. It took three revelations and the consistent witness of these four Hebrew courtiers to bring this king to a worship response to God as his God, and it generally takes more than a single act of revelation to bring us to worship, too.

When Daniel was preserved in the den of lions, King Darius wrote, "I make a decree that in every dominion of my kingdom men must tremble and fear before the God of Daniel. For He is the living God, and steadfast forever" (Dan. 6:26,27). Consistent with his limited spiritual light, Darius sought to produce universal worship of God by decree, but worship is a natural response to a revelation of God. Nevertheless, it was a high-level worship response by a Gentile king.

Daniel met a revealing God, and it produced worship. We, too, must enter into some revelation if we are to be worshippers. We initially need some revelation of ourselves, for most of us live in an image far beneath the image God has of us. Redemption has erased our past and has given us a totally new life, but our memories and fleshly desires tend to cause us to downgrade ourselves rather than to accept God's appraisal of us. For instance, God repeatedly calls us holy, but we consistently speak of ourselves as depraved. God calls us saints, but we call ourselves sinners. We are declared to be children, friends, His body on earth, and kings and priests unto God, but far too often we view ourselves as strangers and pilgrims.

When Nebuchadnezzar saw himself as God saw him— the golden head—he worshipped. So will we! We will worship not as condemned persons seeking pardon but as redeemed, restored and renewed persons who have been granted throne rights. We can "draw near with a true heart in full assurance of faith" (Heb. 10:22).

Of course, we also need some revelation of the person of God, for how can we worship a God we do not know? Since our worship responses will be limited to our revelation of God, we need higher and higher revelations of who God is in order for us to enter into higher and higher levels of worship. Fortunately, God is a self-revealing God who dwells within the worshippers. The entire Bible is God's revelation of Himself to earnest seekers.

God has graciously revealed Himself from Noah through the prophets. It has been progressive revelation that has built upon itself, ever unfolding higher and higher concepts of God. By the time Peter entered into the stream of revelation, he met the God-man and not only walked and talked with Him but lived intimately with Him for nearly three years. He enjoyed what the prophets had deeply yearned for: intimate communion with God.

chapter nine

PETER MET
THE GOD-MAN

"And the Word became flesh and dwelt among us...."
(John 1:14)

Unless divine revelation gives us a fleeting glimpse into the future, none of us parents has the slightest idea of what our children shall become. Scripture does not indicate that such a vision came to Jonah, a fisherman of Galilee. His son, whom he called Simon Bar-Jonah (Simon, son of Jonah), started working in the family business when he was very young. Jesus was the first person to see anything of greatness in this rather ordinary workman of the sea. He called Simon from fishing for fish to fishing for men, for while it was a star that brought the wise men to Jesus, it was fish that brought Simon and Christ together, and on repeated occasions it was fish that formed the object lessons Jesus used to open Simon's eyes to spiritual principles.

From such an inauspicious beginning grew an impulsive, inquisitive, boastful man who sometimes showed timidity and even cowardice. Jesus brought

Simon into fellowship with Himself and began a transformation that started with a name change and ended
in a change of nature—so his impulsiveness became
humility, his inquisitiveness became submission, and
his timid and sometimes cowardly nature became fearless and courageous. In a period of about three years
Jesus changed this man of the nets into a man of God.

Being a man of God, however, is not synonymous
with being appreciated. After the resurrection of Jesus,
the thanks that Peter received from the religious community for performing the mighty miracle of healing
the lame man, who for years had begged at the Beautiful
gate of the temple, was to be arrested and with his companion, John, to spend the night in jail. Brought to trial
before the high priest and Sanhedrin the next day, Peter
and John were threatened and then released, but the tag
this tribunal pinned on to Peter has remained ever since.
The Sanhedrin declared these two men "uneducated and
untrained," or, as the King James Version expresses,
"unlearned and ignorant" (Acts 4:13). Somehow this
evaluation did not stick to John as it has clung to Peter;
to this day people think of Peter as being an ignorant
fisherman.

The basis of this evaluation was probably a comparison. Peter had not enjoyed the formal education that
the members of this high court had received, for Peter's
education had been in his father's fishing business, not
in philosophy and religious law. But the world long ago
learned that wisdom is not always found only among
the educated. Peter possessed both knowledge and wisdom that these learned members of religion's highest
order did not have. From the day of Christ's resurrection until Peter was crucified upside down, Peter's grasp

of divine truths remained a constant conundrum to these scholars. Their rationalization of what they witnessed was "They realized that they [Peter and John] had been with Jesus" (Acts 4:13). What these sages had failed to learn from the scrolls, schools and scribes, Peter and the other disciples learned through their relationship with Jesus Christ.

Peter's Learning Came by Perception

"Ignorant," indeed! Just because another lacks the knowledge that we possess does not make him ignorant. The savage in the jungle possesses survival skills that are totally unknown to most of the professors in our universities. None of us can know everything, nor is it important that all of us know the same thing. Training in crafts is no less an education than training in science, music or philosophy. Society needs both the medical doctor with his scalpel and the brick mason with his trowel. Peter's craft of fishing was as important to his society as farming, for his craft was the source of protein upon which the learned men of his generation depended, and he learned his craft by hands-on experience with his father on the Sea of Galilee.

Peter learned from what he *heard*. As a boy, learning to mend fishing nets on the shores of Galilee, I can imagine he heard about the angelic appearance to a group of shepherds tending their sheep on the hillsides of Bethlehem; he heard the report of the wise men's visit and of the response of Anna and Simeon when Jesus was taken to the temple for His dedication. Palestine is a small country, and young Simon lived less than one hundred miles from Bethlehem and Jerusalem. Furthermore, Nazareth, where Jesus worked with His father in the carpenter shop, was no more than forty miles from the Sea of Galilee. With great wonder young Simon listened to the fishermen's tales about this Jesus whom the angels had declared as Israel's Messiah. Simon's innate inquisitiveness caused him to ask questions, and in the long hours of silence while he was mending nets he turned over and over in his mind the answers he had received.

Years later, when Simon's brother became a follower and disciple of John the Baptist, I imagine Simon was tempted to join him, but the fishing business could hardly lose two workers, so Simon stayed with his father in Galilee. But when Andrew returned home with the report that he had found the Messiah, Simon couldn't resist. He joined Andrew, who "brought him to Jesus. Now when Jesus looked at him, He said, 'You are Simon the son of Jonah. You shall be called Cephas' (which is translated, A Stone)" (John 1:42). Simon Peter was never the same again.

It was not long before Jesus came to Galilee and called Peter away from fishing to become a full-time disciple. As one of the twelve, Peter listened to Jesus talk to the multitudes who flocked to be near Him, and at other times he sat quietly and listened to private conversations Jesus had with inquirers and challengers. He was not in a classroom, and none of our modern teaching aids was available, but Peter was learning. The Scriptures he had memorized as a young boy in the synagogue now came alive as he listened to this man teach. Whatever pedagogical disciplines were lacking were more than compensated for by the inspiration and illumination Jesus brought to His discourses and daily discussions.

But Peter learned not only from what he heard; he

gained a wealth of spiritual knowledge from what he *saw*. From the beginning of his association with Jesus, Peter saw Him as a miracle-worker. Peter was a little skeptical when Jesus performed His first miracle—turning the water into wine at Cana's wedding feast—for Israel had not known an anointed prophet for several hundred years, and the religious institution taught that the day of miracles was past. But this first miracle was followed by a succession of others that were mind-boggling. Jesus opened blind eyes—something that had never been done in the Old Testament. He healed multitudes of sick people. He cured lepers. He caused the lame to walk. He fed thousands with a boy's lunch. Peter was amazed that this Jesus broke up every funeral He attended by restoring the dead to life. What an amazing man! Where did He get this power?

Sometimes Jesus was more a deliverer than a miracle-worker, for He cast out demons with a word of authority. Deaf-mutes both heard and spoke after evil spirits had been cast out of them, and the demoniac of Gadarea was restored to sanity after the legion of demons was transferred from him to the herd of swine. Sometimes these demons cried out, calling Jesus the "Son of the Most High God" (Mark 5:7), and Jesus always made them be silent. Were the demons teasing this greatly anointed man, or was it possible that they actually knew something of the origins of Jesus that mere humans did not yet know?

Neither Peter nor the other disciples could understand the tremendous authority with which Christ both spoke and functioned. All nature seemed to obey Him instantly, for He calmed a storm, walked on water, turned water into wine, multiplied loaves and fish, and even killed a fig tree with a sentence of doom. The priests, scribes and Pharisees all sought to catch Him in His doctrine by asking Him trick questions, but Jesus always confounded them with His answers. His authority in the Word of God was almost beyond belief. It was reported that even at age twelve He had amazed the temple teacher of the Law with His insightful questions.

Of course some of the Old Testament prophets, such as Elijah and Elisha, seemed to have knowledge about events before they happened, but this Jesus projected an awareness of the future that was uncanny, and He even seemed to know what was in people's hearts. Wasn't this just the carpenter's son from Nazareth? He had no ecclesiastical authority or scholastic eminence, and He was without any political power whatsoever; yet He seemed to have authority over everything from an untrained donkey, upon which He rode triumphantly into Jerusalem, to men and women from all walks of life. Peter admired this, but it was a source of much questioning among the disciples.

It wasn't just what Jesus did that amazed Peter; it was the very nature of the man that impressed him so greatly. How could one with such power and authority be so humble and meek? He didn't seem to force Himself upon anyone; to the contrary, He constantly fled from the popularity that built up around Him. He spent long nights in solitary prayer, and He frequently retired into uninhabited places just to talk with the twelve disciples when He could have been teaching the multitudes.

Furthermore, everyone seemed to be comfortable around Him, and He was as equally at ease with children as with the wealthy. He was relaxed in the presence of women, but He was also a "man's man" as well.

Neither the company of sinners nor the questions of unlearned people bothered Him. As a matter of fact, Jesus seemed to get upset only with religious hypocrisy. What a man! Peter learned much from what he saw in Jesus, for years later he wrote, "We...were eyewitnesses of His majesty" (2 Pet. 1:16). What he saw made a lasting impression on his life.

"Ignorant" Peter also learned much from what he personally experienced, for Jesus often let His disciples "get in on the act." The two times Jesus fed the multitudes with just a handful of food, Peter helped hand out the loaves and fish. He was one of seventy sent out to preach the gospel, heal the sick and cast out devils. What he had observed, he was now performing. Peter supplied his boat as a platform from which Jesus taught, and then at Jesus' command caught more fish with one cast of his net than several boats could handle. With Jesus' permission He walked on the water and he was the only disciple whom Jesus personally restored to fellowship after His resurrection. Peter was more than an eyewitness; he was a participant with Jesus. We might say that he received "hands-on" training.

Peter's Knowledge Centered on a Person

Peter concentrated not only on the precepts that were being taught but on the One who taught them. Often after a session of sharing parables with the multitudes, Jesus would find a quiet place to explain the spiritual meaning of the stories that had thrilled the people, but Peter was not filling a notebook with outlines—he was studying the speaker all the time. To comprehend His teaching was one thing, but to understand this Jesus was quite another. As a businessman, Peter was used to sizing up persons, but he had difficulty sizing up this man.

In his Gospel (the early Christian fathers are unanimous in testifying that Mark wrote under Peter's superintendence and by his authority) Peter recorded the incident of Jesus stilling the storm that was about to swamp the boat. Because they were afraid of the storm Peter and the other disciples had angrily awakened Jesus and charged Him with unconcern. But after Jesus had rebuked the wind and calmed the storm, the disciples "feared exceedingly, and said to one another, 'Who can this be, that even the wind and the sea obey Him!' " (Mark 4:41). Peter's fear of the sea was nothing compared to his subsequent fear of Jesus. "Who can this be?" he cried. The King James Version translates the Greek as "What *manner* of man is this?" (emphasis added). Peter and the disciples were looking for a category into which Jesus would fit—with which they were familiar—for if we can classify people, we know how to deal with them. Neither Peter nor the other disciples could find a category sufficiently adequate to capture the person of Jesus. He was in a class by Himself.

Talk about a one-of-a-kind! That phrase could have been coined to describe Jesus. Peter had never encountered a man like this one. In his fishing business Peter had met Greeks, Romans, Samaritans and a few Egyptians, but he had never met anyone with power like this. Jesus was an unfolding mystery to Peter, as He has been to millions of people since then. Unless we accept His proclamation of deity, we will always lack a classification for Him. He is unique and incomparable. Jesus stands alone—from the manner of His birth to His ascension into heaven—and yet He was so much like other men that most of the time Peter was comfortable

around Him. What a composite: natural but supernatural, earthly but spiritual. After nearly three years
of association with Jesus, Peter still could not "pigeon-
hole" Him.

Toward the end of His ministry on earth "when Jesus
came into the region of Caesarea Philippi, He asked His
disciples, saying, 'Who do men say that I, the Son of
Man, am?' So they said, 'Some say John the Baptist,
some Elijah, and others Jeremiah or one of the prophets.' He said to them, 'But who do you say that I am?'
And Simon Peter answered and said, 'You are the
Christ, the Son of the living God' " (Matt. 16:13-16).

Peter had examined the major classifications others
had used for Jesus, but he was not satisfied with them.
He could not put his friend in the prophetic office with
Jeremiah, although even His enemies testified, "No man
ever spoke like this Man!" (John 7:46). Neither was
he content to associate Jesus with Elijah the miracle-
worker, or with John the Baptist, whose life-style Jesus
seemed to follow. In many ways Jesus was all of these
and even more. It was that missing "extra" for which
Peter groped. To his amazement, when Jesus asked,
"Who do you say that I am?," something happened to
Peter. Inner illumination caused all that he had heard,
seen and experienced to crystallize into a grand revelation. An inner voice almost screamed, "You are the
Christ, the Son of the living God!" In that moment of
divine revelation, Peter met the God-man.

Peter's Comprehension Supernaturally Produced

Peter's confession was not the product of deduction;
it was a revelation that exceeded what was natural. It
was inexplicable by ordinary means. It was truly supernatural. Jesus Himself indicated this when He responded

to Peter's confession with the words "Blessed are you, Simon Bar-Jonah, for flesh and blood has not revealed this to you, but My Father who is in heaven" (Matt. 16:17).

Divine revelations are permanent and unchanging. When the Gospel of Mark was being written, Peter insisted on the introductory statement "The beginning of the gospel of Jesus Christ, the Son of God" (Mark 1:1). He certainly was not the only man to declare that Jesus was the "Son of God," but he was the first. Gabriel had made this declaration (see Luke 1:35), the devil acknowledged this claim (see Matt. 4:3,6), and demons attested it (see Matt. 8:29), but Peter was the first of the apostles to receive this revelation. Later John declared it (see John 20:31; 1 John 3:8; Rev. 2:18); Paul widely proclaimed Jesus to be the Son of God (see Rom. 2:4; 2 Cor. 1:19; Gal. 2:20; Eph. 4:13); the entire first chapter of the book of Hebrews is devoted to proving this declaration; and of course Christ Himself verified this claim (see John 10:36; Luke 22:70).

Although divine revelations are permanent, the recipient is often subjected to inner doubts following such illuminations. Peter was no exception. Immediately following Peter's great confession of the deity of Jesus, the God-man began to talk about being killed by the chief priests and elders. This did not fit Peter's new concept (how could God die?) so he rebuked Jesus, saying, " 'Far be it from You, Lord; this shall not happen to You!' But He [Jesus] turned and said to Peter, 'Get behind Me, Satan! You are an offense to Me, for you are not mindful of the things of God, but the things of men' " (Matt. 16:22,23).

In but a few brief hours Peter had been both blessed

and cursed by Jesus. He was first called Peter, a piece of the rock which would be the foundation of the church, and then was called Satan who brought offense to Jesus. It confused Peter, and it affected the clear-cut picture of Jesus as the Christ. Was He man or God?

Jesus the Man

Jesus *came as a man*, for His coming was not by invasion but by involvement. He was conceived in Mary's womb by action of the Holy Spirit, and His gestation and birth were similar to ours. He was circumcised as an infant and taught as a child, and He matured into manhood like thousands of others in His generation. The sacred record declares that "Jesus increased in wisdom and stature, and in favor with God and men" (Luke 12:52). This mental, physical, spiritual and social growth was not dispatched from heaven; it was developed on earth. It was not a gift, nor was it a growth that came mysteriously. It came through maturation. Jesus Christ was a man who began as a baby and developed fully into a man, even though He knew that He was God.

Jesus was *accepted as a man* from the beginning of His ministry. He was received as a man by the laborers as well as by the learned theologians. Children bypassed the disciples to get to Jesus, for they enjoyed His presence and His blessing. So outstanding was His manhood that the Bible calls Him "the last Adam" and "the second Man" (see 1 Cor. 15:45,47). He was what God had made Adam to be before sin marred and scarred that creation. Jesus Christ came without the scars of sin and showed the earth what a person can actually be.

Jesus even *called Himself a man*. If anyone ever lived who had a balanced self-awareness, it was the Lord Jesus

191

Christ. Every word He taught, every miracle He performed and every experience of fellowship He entered into reflected His awareness that He knew what He was doing and why He was doing it. Christ never lost sight of who He was or that He was here from heaven on a special mission, yet He repeatedly called Himself a man. At least fifteen times in the Gospel of Mark He called Himself "the Son of Man," and in the Gospel of John, which is the Gospel that emphasizes the divinity of Christ, Jesus called Himself "the Son of Man" eleven or more times.

Jesus thoroughly knew His divinity, but He constantly spoke of His humanity. Even His heavenly Father acknowledged His humanity, for on the day of Pentecost, Peter proclaimed, "Men of Israel, hear these words: Jesus of Nazareth, a Man attested by God to you..." (Acts 2:22).

Jesus *ministered as a man*, for Peter's sermon continued, "...a Man attested by God to you by miracles, wonders, and signs which God did through Him in your midst, as you yourselves also know" (Acts 2:22). Peter well understood that Jesus ministered by power derived from God rather than by inherent power. It was God working through Him rather than Jesus working as God. Jesus had stepped out of His divine rank to function as a human.

Theologians have coined the word *kenosis* to describe this self-emptying and self-limitation of Christ Jesus. It is not that Christ ceased to be God; it is merely that He laid aside the exercise of His deity, limiting Himself to the resources that are available to all redeemed people. This is among the reasons He dared to tell His disciples, "Most assuredly, I say to you, he who believes in Me, the works that I do he will do also; and greater works than these he will do, because I go to My Father" (John 14:12). Because He chose to function as a man, He challenged others to minister as He had ministered.

Jesus was *subject to the limitations of man*, as Peter well knew. Peter had seen Jesus weary at Jacob's well, angry at the money-changers in the temple, compassionate with the multitude and troubled over the unbelief of His own disciples. Jesus was, indeed, subject to the limitations of humanity. He got hungry, thirsty and tired, and at times He had to get away from the crowd to rest. Even after His resurrection He declared that He was not a spirit but that He had flesh and bones, and in the presence of His disciples He ate a piece of fish to show them that He was still man—in a resurrected body, an eternal body somehow—but still truly man.

Jesus *died as a man*. The sentence of the Law was "The soul who sins shall die" (Ezek. 18:4,20). Since this was a divine decree, it could not be merely set aside; there was no other sentence for sin, and God could not excuse sin and remain just. God's answer was to take the place of the sinner, in Jesus, and die the death that transgressors deserve, thereby releasing the sinner and satisfying the divine statute.

The proposal was idealistic, but the problem seemed insurmountable, for God cannot die. To overcome this barrier, God became a man who not only could die but must die, for he was under the sentence of death. By becoming man and accepting God's sentence for sin, Jesus the God-man became Jesus the Redeemer. The angel told Joseph that Mary would "bring forth a Son, and you shall call His name Jesus, for He will save His people from their sins" (Matt. 1:21), and Paul wrote from the other side of the cross, "Christ has redeemed us from the curse of the law, having become a curse for us (for it is written, 'Cursed is everyone who hangs on a tree')" (Gal. 3:13).

It is, of course, absolutely correct to say that "Jesus Christ hung on the cross as very God of very God," but it was the man Jesus who was arrested, tried, mocked, beaten and forced to drag His cross to Calvary. It was human wrists and ankles that felt the pain of the intruding nails as He was impaled upon the cross. His human head throbbed with the poisonous crown of thorns, and when the soldiers pierced that human side, blood and water gushed out. It was the *man* Christ Jesus who went to Golgotha's brow, but He was always very God of very God.

Jesus came, lived, ministered and died as a man— the perfect man. He was virgin-born; His life was victorious; and His death was vicarious. Furthermore, Jesus Christ is not merely the God-man of history but is equally the God-man of eternity, for He ascended in a glorified body to take His place at the right hand of God on high as our personal representative. As Paul put it, "There is one God and one Mediator between God and men, the Man Christ Jesus, who gave Himself a ransom for all" (1 Tim. 2:5,6).

Jesus the God

Peter had become quite familiar with Jesus the man, but by divine inspiration he had just declared this Jesus to be God. Yet his rational mind could not accept the conflict between what he had seen and what the Spirit had revealed, so, perhaps to impress this revelation indelibly upon him, the event in the life of Jesus that is recorded right after Peter's confession is the transfiguration. Jesus took Peter, James and John "up on a high mountain by themselves, and was transfigured before them. His face shone like the sun, and His clothes became as white as the light" (Matt. 17:1,2).

What had been an inner illumination was now an outer enlightenment. The perception of Peter's spirit was now matched with the experience of his senses. Peter was looking at a manifestation of the *shekinah* that had so stirred Ezekiel to worship. God had shown Ezekiel that the *shekinah* which he saw leave the temple and the holy city would return to a very special temple in the future. Now Peter was looking at both that "temple" and the manifest presence of God in the form of the *shekinah*. God was right there in the midst of them. Wasn't that what Isaiah the prophet had declared? "Behold, the virgin shall conceive and bear a Son, and shall call His name Immanuel" (Is. 7:14). Immanuel—God with us. This had been the hope of Israel for hundreds of years, and here He was—Jesus the Christ. Immanuel! But how? Why?

Every relationship among peoples of this earth has to pall and become prosaic when compared to God's relationship with humanity. The first chapter of the Bible clearly teaches that we were created to be the object with whom God could have intimate fellowship, but sin separated us from our God, and the Bible is a record of God's attempt to bridge the gap that sin engendered. While God successfully established a relationship with a few individuals, the affinities were few and far between, as we have seen. God wanted more. God became human so we could relate to Him in a loving, open, ongoing way. During His brief visit to earth, this God-man was called Jesus. After His ascension He was called

Christ Jesus. Peter stood in the manifest presence of the Christ.

The clear declaration of the Bible is that *Christ Jesus is fully God*. Isaiah prophesied, "For unto us a Child is born [fully man], unto us a Son is given [fully God];...and His name will be called...Mighty God, Everlasting Father..." (9:6). When Paul was writing to the church about Jesus, he proclaimed, "For in Him dwells all the fullness of the Godhead bodily" (Col. 2:9), and in each of his epistles Paul called Jesus "Lord," the Old Testament euphemism for the sacred name of God, which the Jews considered too hallowed to be pronounced openly. "Jesus Christ is Lord" was the essential message of the early church. "Jesus is God!" was their declaration. The Jews in authority considered this heretical, for they had crucified Jesus after charging Him with blasphemy for claiming that He was God, but to the believers this was an indisputable truth. They were convinced that they had met God in the person of Jesus Christ. Were they deluded, or were they enlightened? Look at what they had discovered!

Christ was active in creation, for in the prologue to his Gospel, John wrote, "All things were made through Him, and without Him nothing was made that was made" (John 1:3). That the "Him" refers to Jesus is verified by the context, for the entire chapter is concerned with the coming of Jesus into the world. Christ was active in all of creation.

Paul wrote similarly in his letter to the church in Corinth, saying, "There is only one God, the Father, of whom are all things, and we for Him; and one Lord Jesus Christ, through whom are all things, and through whom we live" (1 Cor. 8:6). Both writers assure us that Jesus Christ was God's divine agent in the creation of everything. This is strong evidence of His deity, for we always ascribe creation to God.

The reality that *Christ Jesus was born as God's Son* is the heart of the Galatian letter. "But when the fullness of the time had come," Paul wrote, "God sent forth His Son, born of a woman, born under the law" (Gal. 4:4). This confirms the message of the angel Gabriel when he appeared to Mary. "Then the angel said to her, 'Do not be afraid, Mary, for you have found favor with God. And behold, you will conceive in your womb and bring forth a Son, and shall call His name JESUS. He will be great, and will be called the Son of the Highest' " (Luke 1:30-32). The supernatural events that accompanied His birth are also confirmation that Christ Jesus the creator was born the creature without losing His status as the Son of God. What a mystery that the author of all life was given life through the process of birth.

Furthermore, *Christ was recognized as God*. The worship of Jesus by the wise men and the shepherds proved that they recognized Him as God. When Jesus was presented in the temple for circumcision, Simeon the prophet recognized God in the Child and cried out, "For my eyes have seen Your salvation which You have prepared before the face of all peoples" (Luke 2:30,31). Even the Roman centurion who was in charge of the crucifixion of Jesus admitted His divinity, for we read, "Now when the centurion, who stood opposite Him, saw that He cried out like this and breathed His last, he said, 'Truly this Man was the Son of God!' " (Mark 15:39).

At least twice during Christ's ministry God said, "This is My beloved Son," as a divine affirmation of

Christ's Sonship: at the beginning of Christ's ministry when Jesus submitted to water baptism, and at the close of His ministry, on the Mount of Transfiguration. God the Father publicly recognized Jesus as God the Son so that all the world could know that Jesus Christ is Lord.

Christ's birth, life, ministry and death all caused men to recognize that He was indeed God. The church at Rome was thrilled to read Paul's affirmation that "Christ came, who is over all, the eternally blessed of God. Amen" (Rom. 9:5). Indeed, the divinity of Christ is the theme of the epistles!

Peter could not have missed that *divine attributes were ascribed to Christ*. In attempting to define the nature of God, we usually speak of the essential attributes of God as being His omnipotence, omniscience, omnipresence, eternity and holiness. These are qualities possessed by God alone, for none other has all power, knows all things, is everywhere present, has always been and is completely holy.

During His brief span on earth, Christ Jesus evidenced all of these essential attributes. He declared His *omnipotence* in saying, "All power is given unto me in heaven and in earth" (Matt. 28:18, KJV). He displayed *omniscience* "because He knew all men, and had no need that anyone should testify of man, for He knew what was in man" (John 2:24,25). As to *omnipresence*, He told His disciples, "Where two or three are gathered together in My name, I am there in the midst of them" (Matt. 18:20). His *eternity* was evidenced in that He was the possessor and imparter of eternal life (see 1 John 5:11,12), and His *holiness* was manifested in His lifestyle and was declared in the prayer of Peter and John when they spoke of "Your holy Servant Jesus, whom

You anointed...that signs and wonders may be done
through the name of Your holy Servant Jesus'' (Acts
4:27,30).

Jesus was fully aware of His *oneness with the Father*.
He stated, ''I came forth from the Father and have come
into the world. Again, I leave the world and go to the
Father'' (John 16:28), thus declaring both His true origin
and His destination. He said further, ''If anyone loves
Me, he will keep My word; and My Father will love
him, and We will come to him and make Our home with
him'' (John 14:23), thereby putting Himself in such
union with the Father that He dared speak of the Father
in the singular and then immediately shift to the plural
We and Our.

On repeated occasions Jesus said that He was in the
Father (see John 14:11,20), and at least once He clearly
declared, ''I and My Father are one'' (John 10:30).
Either Christ was a fraud, was deluded or was actually
God—for He declared that fact and died rather than re-
nounce it. When John, the author of the Gospel that
records the many times Jesus declared His unity with
the Father, wrote his first epistle, he said, ''He who
acknowledges the Son has the Father also'' (1 John
2:23). The inseparableness of the Godhead was as real
to John the aged one as it had been to John the youth.

The fact that *Christ was received as God and will
return as God* also attests to His deity. The resurrection and ascension of Christ Jesus have consistently been
held as proof positive that God accepted Christ's work
and His claims. Paul wrote, ''It is Christ who died, and
furthermore is also risen, who is even at the right hand
of God, who also makes intercession for us'' (Rom.
8:34), and the book of Hebrews declares that ''Christ

has not entered the holy places made with hands, which are copies of the true, but into heaven itself, now to appear in the presence of God for us" (Heb. 9:24). He entered into heaven not as a mere believer but as the second person of the holy Trinity.

Christ Jesus said that He was God, He functioned as God, He was received into heaven as God, and He shall return as God. The angels who accompanied Jesus in the ascension testified, "This same Jesus, who was taken up from you into heaven, will so come in like manner as you saw Him go into heaven" (Acts 1:11), and Paul encouraged us to anticipate "the blessed hope and glorious appearing of our great God and Savior Jesus Christ" (Titus 2:13). Jesus Christ the Lord was fully God every minute He lived here on the earth, and He is God throughout all eternity.

That Peter eventually resolved his conflict between how Jesus could be man and equally be God is seen in his second epistle: "For we did not follow cunningly devised fables," he wrote, "when we made known to you the power and coming of our Lord Jesus Christ, but were eyewitnesses of His majesty. For He received from God the Father honor and glory when such a voice came to Him from the Excellent Glory: 'This is My beloved Son, in whom I am well pleased.' And we heard this voice which came from heaven when we were with Him on the holy mountain" (2 Pet. 1:16-18). The manifestation of the *shekinah* quickened faith in Peter to believe what he could not explain. Even the brilliant scholar Paul made no effort to explain this mystery. He accepted it as a fact, stating succinctly, "Great is the mystery of godliness: God was manifest in the flesh" (1 Tim. 3:16).

Peter's Training Was Practical

God manifested Himself in human flesh to this "ignorant" fisherman who lacked a theological degree or ecclesiastical office. Much like Adam, Peter walked and talked with God on a one-to-one basis every day for nearly three years. Noah and the prophets heard God's voice, but Peter heard, saw and felt God in Jesus Christ. Even the most visionary of the prophets caught only fleeting glimpses of a manifestation of God, and then they were terrified, but this time God chose to manifest Himself in a nonthreatening way by becoming a man. God's goal had always been fellowship, not fear projection, but when He spoke from heaven, people requested that He never speak that way again. When He appeared as an angel, people expected to die; when He came in vision form, people failed to understand what they saw—so God condescended to meet His creation at its own level.

Peter met the God-man, and when spiritual illumination caused him to see beyond the great man—Jesus—to the wonderful God—Christ—his life was transformed forever. He himself became a miracle-worker, following the pattern he had seen in Jesus Christ. He was the first apostle to the Gentiles; he supervised the writing of the first Gospel, he later wrote two epistles. He was a fearless preacher of Jesus Christ who endured repeated imprisonments because he preached what he had experienced. Peter put into practice what he had learned, and he had a passion to cause others to know what he now knew: that "Jesus Christ is Lord."

Not only was Peter practical in his private application of his relationship with Jesus, but in his first epistle he also made some very practical applications to our personal behavior. Realizing that comparatively few persons had shared his intimate relationship with Jesus Christ, he wrote, "...whom having not seen you love. Though now you do not see Him, yet believing, you rejoice with joy inexpressible and full of glory" (1 Peter 1:8), and he further suggested that this faith, "though it is tested by fire, may be found to praise, honor, and glory at the revelation of Jesus Christ" (1 Peter 1:7). Peter was convinced that the good news of the God-man should inspire joyful praise.

He was right, you know, for one of the things the coming of Jesus Christ accomplished was the restoration of joy in the hearts of believers. The religion of Christ's day was burdensome and sorrowful, much as is most religion in our day. People were, and are, laden with rules, regulations, rituals and observations that were not only obligatory but were fear-inducing. There was no joy, for the heart of all religious systems is guilt, and the guilty soul cannot experience real joy. Jesus came to demonstrate God's love and to remit all our guilt to His account, which He paid in full at Calvary. In coming to us as one of us, He successfully introduced us to the Father. He helped us see beyond God's austere, judgmental nature, which seems to dominate the Old Testament revelation, and to see a concerned, loving Father who, for thousands of years, has missed a close association with the people of His love.

Peter declared that the coming of the God-man enabled God to make us a special people whose purpose of existence is joyful response to God. He wrote, "But you are a chosen generation, a royal priesthood, a holy nation, His own special people, that you may proclaim the praises of Him who has called you out of darkness into His marvelous light; who once were not a people but are now the people of God" (1 Pet. 2:9,10). God became a person so that He could make us become "the people of God." Christ took on our nature so that we could be partakers of His nature, as Peter realized: "His divine power has given to us all things that pertain to life and godliness...that...you may be partakers of the divine nature" (2 Peter 1:3,4). The God-man—Jesus Christ—enables us to be men and women of God. What joyful responses of praise and worship this should produce!

John, who shared Peter's derogatory label, "ignorant men," also gloried in the reality of the transformation of man's nature that has come to us since Christ became one with us. He wrote, "Behold what manner of love the Father has bestowed on us, that we should be called children of God!... Beloved, now we are children of God; and it has not yet been revealed what we shall be, but we know that when He is revealed, we shall be like Him, for we shall see Him as He is" (1 John 3:1,2). John, too, knew the God-man, but his appraisal of what he saw was that "God is love" (1 John 4:8). Both men saw Jesus as God's Christ, but John also saw Him as God's love made flesh. John met a loving God.

chapter ten

JOHN MET A LOVING GOD

"...God is love."

(1 John 4:8)

I have always been interested in observing how differently people view the same set of circumstances. When I served on a jury some years ago, I was amazed by the contrasting and often conflicting testimony of the witnesses. There was no reason to believe that anyone was lying; it was simply that each person saw the incident from a different perspective and filtered it through his or her particular mind-set.

This principle is clearly seen in Peter and John. Both were disciples of Jesus, both ministered with and for the Christ, and both saw the same miracles and heard the same teachings, but each of them assessed the circumstances differently. Peter saw the God-man, while John saw the nature of God in the man. Peter spoke of faith bringing us into an abundant "knowledge of our Lord Jesus Christ" (2 Pet. 1:8), while John wrote, "By this we know love, because He laid down His life for us'' (1 John 3:16). Peter never lost his perspective of having seen the person of Christ, while John constantly referred to the light and love of the nature of Christ. Neither is a complete picture of Christ Jesus, but taken together they show the nature of man and the nature of God blended magnificently.

Perhaps the variant viewpoints are rooted in the different natures of these men. Peter, the fisherman, was a "people person" whom Jesus called to be a "fisher of men," while John was described as the great apostle of love and even spoke of himself as "the disciple whom Jesus loved" (John 21:20). John was the mystic, the seer, the man of foresight to whom the great apocalyptic vision of the book of Revelation was given. It is to be expected, then, that these two men would have differing views of Jesus the Christ.

Descending Love

This divergence of views is evident at the very beginning of John's Gospel. Matthew gives the genealogy of Christ through the lineage of Joseph, and tells about the appearance of the angel to Joseph and, later, the visit of the Magi; Luke traces the genealogy of Jesus through the lineage of Mary and describes Gabriel's visit to Mary and the angelic chorus's announcement of this miraculous birth to the shepherds; but John begins his Gospel by giving the divine lineage of Jesus. He wrote, "In the beginning was the Word, and the Word was with God, and the Word was God. He was in the beginning with God. And the Word became flesh and dwelt among us..." (John 1:1,2,14). "The Word...dwelt among us" became the skeletal structure upon which John hung his Gospel.

Matthew and Luke were concerned with the persons

involved in the birth of Jesus, but John's mind turned to the reason Christ was born. He made the powerful declaration that "God so loved the world that He gave His only begotten Son, that whoever believes in Him should not perish but have everlasting life" (John 3:16). John did not see humanity's condition as the motivating force behind the divine incarnation; he saw God's divine love as the impelling power of the incarnation. In his first epistle John wrote, "God is love. In this the love of God was manifested toward us, that God has sent His only begotten Son into the world, that we might live through Him" (1 John 4:8,9).

As John viewed it, the secret of Christ's coming was two-fold: It declared God's love for us, and it demonstrated His willingness to show that love to us. Love seeks to express itself in gifts that will show forth its nature and that will best satisfy those it loves. God's moral love would have been forever unknown to us if He had not expressed it in a way that we could understand. John caught sight of this; immediately after declaring, "God is love," he added, "In this the love of God was manifested toward us, that God has sent His only begotten Son into the world." This is not, of course, the *only* manifestation of God's love, for the world and our lives abound with evidences of His love, but the coming of Christ Jesus was the *supreme* manifestation of divine love, and without it we would not know how to interpret the other exhibitions of God's love. The heavens declare the glory of God; His actions reveal His grace; nature shows His handiwork, but in Christ Jesus we meet God's *demonstrated* love. There is no other proof of the love of the Father equal to this: Christ, the Son of God, came to sinful people to compensate us for our inability to see the invisible God.

In his *Expositions of Holy Scripture*, Alexander Maclaren writes, "Before Jesus Christ came into this world no one ever dreamt of saying, 'God *loves.*' Some of the Old Testament psalmists had glimpses of that truth and came pretty near expressing it. But among all the 'gods many and lords many,' there were lustful gods and beautiful gods, and idle gods, and fighting gods and peaceful gods: but not one of whom worshippers said, 'He loves.' 'God loves' is the greatest thing that can be said by lips" (Volume 10).

John's declaration that "God is love" defines God's essential nature in the highest conception we humans can hold. It forces us to believe that the divine love is eternal and unchangeable—it is "that which was from the beginning" (1 John 1:1)—and it requires us to believe that His love governs all other attributes in the Godhead, for to say, "God is love," implies that all His activity is loving activity. God rules in love; He chastens in love; He relates to us in love. Furthermore, this revelation makes us aware that God's love to humanity originated entirely with Himself, and that God is the fountain of all love. "Love is of God...God is love," John wrote (1 John 4:7,8).

The apostle continued, "In this is love, not that we loved God, but that He loved us and sent His Son to be the propitiation for our sins" (1 John 4:10). The incarnation and atonement constitute the revelation of God's love. John's contemporaries saw the persons who were involved in the incarnation and the trappings that surrounded it, but John saw the love of God manifested in that event. He saw the full being of God's nature as present in Jesus. While other values in life can imitate God's love, only Jesus actually and fully communicates that love. Ultimately the only safe ground for believing and asserting that God is love is His self-revelation in Christ.

Ministering Love

As surely as God's love was the impelling power of Christ's incarnation, so it was the dynamic force in Christ's ministry. While it is easy for us to speak of Christ's compassion for the sick and His empathy for the enslaved, it is inaccurate for us to project these as the motivating factors in Christ's outstanding ministry. He was impelled by God's love, not by people's need. He did not come merely to alleviate the results of sin in a few people in Palestine; He came to destroy the power of sin for people of every nation. John said of Jesus, "For this purpose the Son of God was manifested, that He might destroy the works of the devil" (1 John 3:8). The Greek word he used for destroy is *luo*, which basically means "to come unglued, to loose, or to cause to lose consistency."

This loosing of which *luo* speaks is like that which happens when mortar becomes rotten and crumbles so that a brick building slowly disintegrates. It is like a beautifully handcrafted chair whose joints slip apart because the glue used in its construction has decomposed and lost its adhesive powers. It is like a woman's sewing if the bobbin runs out of thread. All of the pieces remain, but they lack any cohesive force to keep them together.

Christ came not to destroy the devil at this time but to "destroy the *works* of the devil"—to make everything he had built crumble and break down. A frontal attack

209

might have left many human casualties; instead He released the human captives bound by sin. Before Christ came, sin had dominion over people, but God's love sent Jesus to break the power of sin and to give the dominion back to redeemed persons, so that the Word dares to declare, "Sin shall not have dominion over you" (Rom. 6:14). John put it in a positive form in saying, "Whatever is born of God overcomes the world. And this is the victory that has overcome the world—our faith. Who is he who overcomes the world, but he who believes that Jesus is the Son of God?" (1 John 5:4,5). What a demonstration of divine love that the former slaves become the masters.

Christ's mission was to reveal God's love, and John caught sight of this. While the synoptic Gospels repeatedly report the things Jesus did, John wrote of the things Jesus said. He wrote of only seven miracles that Jesus performed, and then he generally used them as audio-visuals to set the stage for Jesus' teaching. John delicately balanced these seven miracles with Christ's seven statements: "I am the bread...the light...the shepherd...the resurrection...the life...the truth...the vine." John stood less in awe of Christ's miracles than of the revelation of His personhood and mission as revealed in His teachings. John recorded more of Christ's discourses than did any other writer in Scripture. Perhaps he sensed that the miracles were attention-getters and attesting signs, but the teaching of Jesus flowed with manifold evidences of God's love.

John does not picture Jesus as offering a cheap love. Jesus taught a tough love—a love that demanded discipline, determination and action. John recorded that Christ's final discourse to His disciples included: "He who has My commandments and keeps them, it is he who loves Me. And he who loves Me will be loved by My Father, and I will love him and manifest Myself to him'' (John 14:21). John did not understand Jesus to be saying that love originates in us, for he clearly stated, ''In this is love, not that we loved God, but that He loved us...'' (1 John 4:10). He heard Jesus say that loving God requires having the commandments *and* keeping them. Obedience to what Christ taught is proof of love, and that love is the inspiration of obedience. We cannot obey that which is unknown, so John saw Jesus as the loving teacher who was paving a pathway for people to love God.

God's love is first demonstrated to us through Christ Jesus, but when we answer that love with observance and obedience, His love is able to flow on toward us, unchecked in its manifestation and operation. There is nothing we can do that will make God stop loving us, but unless we observe and obey we put ourselves in a place where we are not conscious of its power. Disobedience is sin, and sin always impedes the flow of God's love to our lives.

Knowing this, John wrote, ''My little children, these things I write to you, that you may not sin. And if anyone sins, we have an Advocate with the Father, Jesus Christ the righteous'' (1 John 2:1). Sin separates us from the flow of God's love, but Jesus stands between us and God to re-establish that flow. Christ's ministry was to reveal God's love, teach us the way to remain in that love and provide legal recourse for us if we depart from that love. He came to show us God's love, to set us in that love and to secure us in His love.

For all of this, John had to admit, ''He came unto

His own, and His own did not receive Him. But as many as received Him, to them He gave the right to become children of God, even to those who believe in His name" (John 1:11,12). No matter how strong love is, that love remains powerless to effect a change unless there is a response to it. Christ demonstrated and taught God's love, but He could not force people to respond to and accept that love.

In her book *Those Who Love Him*, Basilea Schlink wrote: "Yet behold Him again, this King and Lord! See Him humble and lowly. He leaves the glory of heaven. He comes to the sons of men, to sinners. They do not want Him, and they will not receive Him. Yet He comes. They hated Him in return. Yet He loves them still. In the end they torture Him to death. They deride and mock. They nail Him to a cross. He loves them.

"Again and again, His words toward them are words of love and compassion. His is a foolish love. A spendthrift love that lavishes love upon those who trample Him under foot. It offers everything."

Revealing Love

A recurring theme in Christ's teaching was His equality with God. He declared that His origin and His authority were from the Father and that He would depart to return to the Father. He sought to convince humanity that the love they sensed flowing from Him was the love of the Father in heaven. In His high priestly prayer He announced, "I have declared to them Your name, and will declare it, that the love with which You loved Me may be in them, and I in them" (John 17:26).

From Adam and Eve's expulsion from Eden until the beginning of the ministry of Christ Jesus, few people thought of God as loving. He was seen as austere, judgmental, powerful and holy, but how could sinful men conceive of God's love—especially of God's love for them? People have consistently looked at themselves to see what God was like, but this has always given them a warped concept of the heavenly Father. God is not as people imagine Him to be; He is who He has revealed Himself to be, and the greatest demonstration was in His Son, Jesus Christ.

Again and again John recorded Jesus' teaching that He and the Father were inseparable. Eight times in the fifth chapter of the Gospel of John, Jesus spoke of His union with the Father. First He said that they work together: "My Father has been working until now, and I have been working" (John 5:17). Second, Jesus said that everything He did was what the Father showed Him to do: "The Son can do nothing of Himself, but what He sees the Father do; for whatever He does, the Son also does in like manner" (John 5:19). Third, Jesus said that He and the Father shared in raising the dead: "As the Father raises the dead and gives life to them, even so the Son gives life to whom He will" (John 5:21). Fourth, Jesus taught that He and the Father shared together in all judgment: "For the Father judges no one, but has committed all judgment to the Son" (John 5:22).

Next, Jesus insisted that "all should honor the Son just as they honor the Father. He who does not honor the Son does not honor the Father who sent Him" (John 5:23). Sixth, Jesus said that both He and the Father have inherent life: "For as the Father has life in Himself, so He has granted the Son to have life in Himself" (John 5:26). Seventh, Jesus affirmed that He always submitted to the will of the Father: "I do not seek My own will but the will of the Father who sent Me" (John 5:30);

and eighth, Jesus spoke of both the Father and Son bearing witness of Jesus (see John 5:32,36).

In short, Jesus claimed a commonality with God in His work, activity, resurrection power, judgment, honor, life, will and witness. Little wonder, then, that He reprimanded the Pharisees, "You know neither Me nor My Father. If you had known Me, you would have known My Father also" (John 8:19), or that He answered Philip's request "Lord, show us the Father, and it is sufficient for us" with the words "Have I been with you so long, and yet you have not known Me, Philip? He who has seen Me has seen the Father; so how can you say, 'Show us the Father?' " (John 14:8, 9).

How long it takes us to see the Father in the Son and to recognize the Son in the Father. They are one! All the tenderness, compassion, forgiveness, caring and love that Jesus demonstrated are equally present in our heavenly Father. Jesus came to make that abundantly clear.

It would not have been sufficient only to declare, "God so loved the world," or "God is love." Words are fragile tools for implanting such dynamic truths into the consciousness of sinners. It took the gift of God Himself in the person of Jesus Christ to make us aware of this divine love. What a gift!—for in giving us Jesus Christ, God gave us Himself. And if God is the great giver, it is because He is the great lover.

Men had imagined Jehovah as a mighty potentate, irresponsible in power, jealous of His own dignity, exacting obedience and praise and sacrifices; but in Christ they saw God willing to seek and to save—ready even, incredible though it might seem, to suffer and agonize

214

for their sakes, loving humanity even in their disobedience and willfulness, and giving Himself for them.

How different is God's love from the emotion that we label love. The love one person has for another is produced by something in the object of that love, something that meets an inherent need. In contrast to this, the love of God is free, spontaneous and uncaused. The only reason God loves any of us is found in His own sovereign will, for He declared, "The Lord did not set His love on you nor choose you because you were more in number than any other people, for you were the least of all peoples; but because the Lord loves you" (Deut. 7:7,8).

Many today talk about the love of God, yet they are total strangers to the God of love, but God cannot be separated from His love, nor can His love be separated from His person. "God is love," and to know the love of God requires knowing God. This was made amazingly simple in the coming of Jesus Christ, for "God...chose us in Him [Jesus] before the foundation of the world, that we should be holy and without blame before Him in love" (Eph. 1:3,4). Chosen in Christ to be in love with God! No wonder the Bible speaks of "His great love with which He loved us" (Eph. 2:4).

In Jesus John saw more than just a Savior. He saw a love that would reveal the true nature of God to people and make it possible for us to respond to God in love instead of in fear and dread.

Sacrificing Love

In his writings, John modestly refrained from referring to himself directly, but he was the disciple who stayed with Jesus throughout the Lord's arrest, trial and crucifixion. He saw the poisonous thorns formed into a crown and pressed into Christ's head, and for years he would hear the swish of the harsh Roman cat-o'-nine-tails as Jesus was scourged at the whipping post. It is likely that John was but a few steps behind Jesus as He wound His way along the Via Dolorosa through Jerusalem to the skull-shaped hill outside the city walls, and there on Golgotha (from the Hebrew), or Calvary (from the Greek), John stood with the mother of Jesus as the cruel Roman spikes were driven through the wrists and ankles of Jesus. He watched in horror as the cross was raised skyward and then dropped into the hole in the earth with such force as to dislodge the arms from their sockets.

John listened to the mocking crowd and the jeers of the soldiers. He marveled as Jesus responded by praying, "Father, forgive them, for they do not know what they do" (Luke 23:34). John saw the love of Jesus extended to a thief hanging on a cross by His side, and he became a participant in that love as Jesus commissioned him to become the providing son for His mother, Mary. Finally, in a triumphant exclamation of love, Jesus cried to the Father, "It is finished!" (John 19:30), and died. Jesus demonstrated His love by giving His life!

Love is demonstrable—how else would we know it is? A very popular syndicated cartoon is titled simply "Love is..." and the cartoonist gives us a daily picture of love, reinforcing that it is a life-style, an attitude expressed or a reaction to an action. While the cartoonist appears to be defining love, he is actually portraying love in life.

In a similar vein, we could say that love is a baby's contented cooing in response to a mother's gentle song—even when that baby is wrapped in swaddling clothes and cradled in a manger. Love is a son's outstretched arms expectantly reaching toward a father as the two of them are reunited—even when those arms are nailed to a rugged cross at Calvary. Love is the expression of words of commitment whereby one lover says to another, "Into Your hands I commend my spirit" (Luke 23:46). Love is unselfish, costly giving that benefits the recipient more than the giver, for "God demonstrates His own love toward us, in that while we were still sinners, Christ died for us" (Rom. 5:8).

Christ died not to make God love us but because God did love His people. Calvary is the supreme demonstration of divine love. Whenever we are tempted to doubt the love of God, we need only to go back to Calvary. It is easy for us to get so involved in the foreshadowing of Christ's death that we lose sight of the magnificent demonstration of divine love that occurred on Golgotha. It is true that a price had to be paid for sin, that a spotless lamb had to be slaughtered, that blood had to be sprinkled, that sin had to be carried away on the scapegoat, but the foundational truth of Christ's death on the cross is "He loved us and sent His Son to be the propitiation for our sins" (1 John 4:10).

Is there a person alive today who can fathom the depths of such love? Can our most learned theologians give us any rational reason for a sinless, holy, eternal, immutable, glorious, moral, almighty God to love such debased, wretched, immoral, rebellious, condemned and hell-bent sinners such as we? Our finite minds cannot grasp the infinite love of an eternal God, but our faith can appropriate it to the changing of our lives. John summarized our proof of God's love for us in these simple words: "By this we know love, because He laid down

217

His life for us" (1 John 3:16).

That God would forgive our sins would be wonder enough, but that He would actually become one of us, vicariously—taking our place as a substitute—to die the death that we deserved so that we could enter into a life we certainly did not deserve, is a wonder of wonders. That will take all of eternity to unravel the mystery. For the present we must accept the limited statement of the Scripture that "God so loved...."

In his first epistle John defined the very essence of God in Christ as being "life," "light" and "love" (see 1:2,5; 4:8). God is, indeed, life—the very source of all life—"dwelling in unapproachable light" (1 Tim. 6:16). Yet at Calvary that life was given up on our behalf, and darkness covered the face of the earth for three hours, all to demonstrate fully that "God is love." Truly "God...gave Himself for our sins..." (Gal. 1:3,4). John reflected upon this: "We have seen and testify that the Father has sent the Son as Savior of the world" (1 John 4:14). Christ's love was certainly a sacrificing love.

Ascending Love

This love of God that descended from the throne to the manger to manifest itself to fallen humanity overflowed with an ascending power that lifts us from the guttermost to the uttermost. John wrote, "In this the love of God was manifested toward us, that God has sent His only begotten Son into the world, that we might live through Him" (1 John 4:9). *Toward us* is not an adequate translation of the Greek. Scholars point out that it actually means "in us" and belongs to "manifested," and many of the modern translations use the term "among us." God's love was manifested in and among us. This brings the experience from the mere objective to include the subjective. It is not God merely displaying His love to the world but actually demonstrating the power of that love in the lives of believing persons.

That divine love was displayed in and among us "that we might live through Him." God chose to share His very nature with us, and He who is love is also life. John made this extremely simple in writing, "And this is the testimony: that God has given us eternal life, and this life is in His Son. He who has the Son has life; he who does not have the Son of God does not have life" (1 John 5:11,12). Jesus, who came as an expression of God's love, is God's source and channel of divine life as certainly as the tree of life was Adam's agent for life. Adam forfeited his access to the tree of life, but God, through sending Jesus, has placed that life within the believers. How much greater and safer is our source than Adam's.

Not only has a source of life been restored to believing persons, but the relationship Adam forfeited in Eden has been reestablished for those who will believe in Jesus. John wrote, "Behold what manner of love the Father has bestowed on us, that we should be called children of God!" (1 John 3:1). All this lavish display of love, unspeakable as it is, has one great end: that people should become, in the deepest sense, His children. The Greek word John chose to use for "children" emphasizes the children's kindred nature with their father. It is not that we are given the honorary title of "children," but we are actually made members of the divine family with the right to call God "Father." Slaves are made children through this ascending love of God, for "as many as received Him, to them He gave the right to become children of God, to those who believe in His name" (John 1:12).

It is worth repeating that this is not a mere declaration but a design of God's perfect will. Seven times in his first epistle John spoke of our being "born of God"—among them, "everyone who practices righteousness is born of Him" (2:29); "everyone who loves is born of God and knows God" (4:7); "whoever believes that Jesus is the Christ is born of God" (5:1). John was saying that by faith, by love and by changed behavior we have become children of God through the new birth.

But John also said that the best is yet to come: "Beloved, now we are children of God; and it has not yet been revealed what we shall be, but we know that when He is revealed, we shall be like Him, for we shall see Him as He is" (3:2). The marvelous ascent in the love of God that John laid before us is like a climb higher and higher up a mountain peak. First we are assured that we are *beloved* of God; then we are informed that we have been *born* of God; next we are guaranteed that "we shall *be like* Him," and finally, we stand on the highest peak of God's promises with the assurance that we shall "*behold* Him as He is." Talk of God's condescending love all you will; there is an ascendance in the love of God that lifts us higher and higher until the image that was lost in Adam is re-formed in the children of God.

Love found us where we were but lifted us to where God is. Love reached us as we were but transformed our nature into God's nature. Love looked upon us in our shame but permitted us to look upon God in His splendor, and "beholding as in a mirror the glory of the Lord, [we] are being transformed into the same image from glory to glory, just as by the Spirit of the Lord'' (2 Cor. 3:18).

Reciprocal Love

''God is love,'' the Bible declares, and therefore we cannot originate love; we can only receive it and dispense it. Since God is the source of love, and Christ is the proof of love, our service can become the expression of love and boldness will be the outcome of love—boldness not merely of service, but boldness in worship. The book of Hebrews declares, ''Therefore, brethren, having boldness to enter the Holiest by the blood of Jesus...let us draw near with a true heart in full assurance of faith...and let us consider one another in order to stir up love and good works'' (Heb. 10:19, 22,24).

Since worship is love responding to love, and since nothing in heaven, on earth or in hell can separate us from God's love, then surely nothing can prevent us from responding to that love, and such response is worship. Worship is an attitude of our hearts reaching toward God with a pouring out of our total self in thanksgiving, praise, adoration and love to God, who created and redeemed us and restored us to full fellowship with Himself.

Perhaps as nearly exact a definition of worship as we can find in the Scriptures came from the lips of Jesus when He said, ''You shall love the Lord your God with all your heart, with all your soul, with all your mind, and with all your strength'' (Mark 12:30). God, made flesh and dwelling among us, declared that the prime fundamental to Christian living is *love*. Love that is received, returned and extended to others becomes the heartbeat of the children of God. We are birthed into a spiritual existence by the love of God, and that love becomes the breath of life in us throughout eternity.

Love that releases all of the heart's adoration, expresses all of the soul's attitudes, explains all of the mind's determination and utilizes all of the strength of the worshipper's body is worship. How far beneath that standard most of the singing praise of church congregations falls, and how critical we are of those who seek to "go all out" in worshipping God, especially if they try to worship Him with body language.

The purest motivation for worship is love that flows out of our spirits like a spring of living water. We need not—indeed, we cannot—originate that love, but we can receive it and let it bubble forth its singing joy to the God who gave us such love.

Worship is far more than awe produced by beautiful architecture or reverence incited by vestments or the sense of sacredness prompted by the sacraments or even the stirred emotions elicited by music. Worship is the interaction of the love in our spirits with the loving nature of the Spirit of God.

We must not be merely recipients of love; we must also be responders to love, for love must be communicated or it will die. John expressed this by saying, "We love Him because He first loved us" (1 John 4:19). Our worship is always a reciprocal response to love received, and in that response we renew our love and our relationship with the object of that love.

Paul understood this, for his farewell to the church in Corinth included the words "the God of love and peace will be with you" (2 Cor. 13:11). He had had a life-changing encounter with this God of love.

chapter eleven

PAUL MET THE INDWELLING GOD

"...Christ in you, the hope of glory."
(Colossians 1:27)

We could hardly find a greater contrast in persons than that which exists between John and Paul. John the beloved was a disciple of John the Baptist, who was a preacher of righteousness and a herald of the coming Christ; Paul, then called Saul, was a disciple of Gamaliel, who was a teacher of the Law and was among the staunch opponents of Jesus. John possessed a gentle, tender spirit; Paul was a thunderous, explosive man who happily resorted to violence to enforce his concepts of right. John was an "unlearned" fisherman; Paul was a highly educated man. John had no position in the religious society; Paul was both a Pharisee and a member of the Sanhedrin. These men were the "East" and "West" of the religious society of Christ's day, and yet each was chosen for a specific task in the church of Jesus Christ.

I've often heard people say that the Lord always

chooses the wrong person for the task He assigns. But that seems the case because "man looks at the outward appearance, but the Lord looks at the heart" (1 Sam. 16:7). Like a master craftsman, God, who "looks at the heart," reaches for the tool that will best do the task at hand, and He feels no compulsion to ask the opinion or permission of any bystanders.

Paul Chosen

In the early church, one of the tools for which God reached was Saul of Tarsus—a most unlikely vessel for divine service. Paul, as he was later known, did not believe that this choice by Jesus was a last-minute decision, for he later wrote, "He chose us in Him before the foundation of the world..." (Eph. 1:4). Paul never conceived of God playing "catch-up" or reacting to any human or demonic action; he always saw God working according to a predetermined plan that was as unvarying as the rising of the morning sun.

God chooses workers according to His predetermined will, but He has to seek out those people, and He often finds them in unusual places and circumstances. Noah was a righteous man in a decadent generation, while Abraham was an idolater in Ur of the Chaldeans. Moses was a runaway murderer hiding as a shepherd in the desert regions of Sinai; Joshua was a Hebrew slave in Egypt who became the servant of Moses. Isaiah was a prophet in the royal court; Ezekiel was a captive in Babylon; Daniel was a government servant in that same country. Peter was a fisherman on the Sea of Galilee, and John had been a disciple of John the Baptist, but Saul of Tarsus was a Pharisee and a theological graduate.

God found each person in a different circumstance.

Only Isaiah the prophet, Ezekiel the priest and Paul the Pharisee came from the religious system, and among them Paul was by far the most religious. He was not only a member of the fundamentalist sect of the Pharisees, but he apparently was also a member of the ruling body, the Sanhedrin.

Paul was not casual about his religion; he was zealous to the point of fanaticism, willing to kill for his faith, and he became the great persecutor of the early Christian church, arresting, imprisoning and slaughtering believers. The Acts of the Apostles tells us, "Then Saul, still breathing threats and murder against the disciples of the Lord, went to the high priest and asked letters from him to the synagogues of Damascus, so that if he found any who were of the Way, whether men or women, he might bring them bound to Jerusalem" (Acts 9:1,2). Vincent translates this as "breathing hard, out of threatening and murderous desire." The use of the word "still" indicates that this was a continuing condition in Saul. He was inflamed with passion, controlled by anger and agitated with indignation to the point that his breath came in gasps and his speech was the raging rantings of a madman. He was a man with a cause, and that cause had become a burning fire in his bosom. Paul set his will to protect God and truth, no matter how much suffering his zeal might cause others.

It is little wonder, then, that the apostles in Jerusalem considered him the number one enemy of the church. He may well have been the theme of many a sermon, and he most certainly was the subject of many prayers, for the church in Damascus was well advised of Saul's intent and priestly authority. Fear and anxiety seemed to block the apostles' minds, keeping them from recognizing in Saul a divine calling that had frustrated him as surely as Moses' calling had caused him to murder an oppressor in an attempt to deliver his people from Egyptian oppression.

The church branded Saul a molester, but God had chosen him as the replacement for Judas—in spite of the vote taken in the Upper Room. How slow we Christians are to realize that God's will is not determined in a ballot box, although occasionally it has been discovered there. Long before Peter called the business meeting that resulted in the election of Matthias as a replacement apostle (see Acts 1:15-26), God had chosen Saul, for Paul wrote, "But when it pleased God, who separated me from my mother's womb and called me through His grace, to reveal His Son in me, that I might preach Him among the Gentiles, I did not immediately confer with flesh and blood" (Gal. 1:15,16). God's calling preceded man's choosing and thus became the choice by divine decree. God's will cannot be overridden by our machinery, no matter how religious that machinery may be.

Paul Confronted

Young Saul must have known something of a divine confrontation, for he became a Pharisee and a seeker after God. His enrollment in the school of Gamaliel, a teacher of the Law, was somewhat like entering theological seminary today. Saul had an undefined passion for God that seemed to defy satisfaction. He sought fulfillment in religious performance, in intellectual pursuit after God and eventually in religious rulership, but none of this satisfied his inner craving. It is likely that this very drive toward God motivated Saul to persecute the fledgling church, as he sincerely felt he was doing God's work.

He was disturbed about the inroads Christianity was making in Jerusalem, and that was greatly intensified by the reports that this doctrine was rapidly reaching beyond the borders of Israel. Damascus, with a Jewish population of some forty thousand who had worshipped in thirty or forty synagogues, had been visited by God's Spirit, and Saul felt that a successful raid at Damascus would be a decisive blow to the new sect and would, perhaps, act as a deterrent to evangelism in other cities.

Armed with arrest warrants and accompanied by soldiers to enforce the arrests, Saul set out over rough, steep roads on the 150-mile journey to Damascus. The heat, dust and drudgery of the journey only intensified Saul's "righteous indignation," and even worse than the boredom of the trip was the inner burning of his conscience. Saul had not only consented to Stephen's death, which means that he gave his vote as a member of the Sanhedrin, but he had actually guarded the coats of the ones who had thrown the fatal stones.

Stephen's conflict was with the Hellenists, not with the Hebrews, and the whole of his marvelous address (Acts 7) was a protest against Hellenism. This deacon's fight was not with the Pharisees but with the Sadducees. Saul's honesty prompted him to admit that he and Stephen had far more in common than they had differences. Stephen was emphasizing the spirituality of religion, claiming that he had seen into the world beyond to behold a living Lord and Master. All of this should have been a vindication of Saul's own philosophy and profoundest conviction. Finally, that gracious, loving, forgiving prayer that Stephen prayed as the stones authorized by Saul were hurled into Stephen's body confronted Saul as he never had before been confronted.

Saul had defeated his opponent with death, but the ideological confrontation continued. Did Saul win over Stephen, or would Stephen's martyrdom eventually win over Saul? Stones of granite are no match for words of prayer.

History has repeatedly confirmed that vehemence is never more violent than when it begins to suspect that it is wrong, and that persecution is never more passionate nor fanaticism more fierce than when it senses the goodness and innocence of its victim. There was not much about the apostles that impressed Saul, but the prayer of one deacon disturbed him immensely. It has been well said that "if Stephen had not prayed, Paul had not preached."

Stephen's suffering ended when stone after stone broke his body, but Saul was wounded a thousand times a day by the words of this first martyr. Saul had plenty of time to grapple with his conscience during the three days he journeyed as the representative of the high priest in Jerusalem, for God did not appear to him until near the end of his journey. Some traditions say that Saul was near the village called Caucab, about ten miles from Damascus, when the light appeared to him, while other traditions say that he was only a quarter of a mile from the gates. Either way, God did not intervene until almost the last moment, as often seems to be the case. God is so completely in charge of situations that He doesn't have to hurry His program.

Saul's ultimate confrontation came when "suddenly a light shone around him from heaven. Then he fell to the ground, and heard a voice saying to him, 'Saul, Saul, why are you persecuting Me?' And he said, 'Who are You, Lord?' And the Lord said, 'I am Jesus, whom you are persecuting. It is hard for you to kick against the goads' '' (Acts 9:3-5). It was one thing to be challenged by Stephen's defense and prayer, but quite another to encounter the divine person of Jesus Christ! This had shifted from an ideological conflict to a personal confrontation, and there was no way Saul could win, for Jesus did not fight with carnal weapons—He struck with light from heaven and a voice addressing the heart and conscience of Saul.

Paul Converted

In the ninth chapter of Acts, Dr. Luke told the story of Paul's conversion, and Paul himself related the experience in chapters 22 and 29. If it was valuable enough to be told three times in one book, one wonders how many times Paul recounted this story during his missionary journeys. It seems that extraordinary conversion is a preparation for extraordinary service. Preachers who have no deep experience to fall back on cannot speak to the deep needs of others. Paul never lacked this. He never doubted his calling from God.

Saul's conversion was both instantaneous and progressive. The moment he called Jesus "Lord," he was saved, but there were still many things in his mind and emotions that needed adjusting. The Greek word that the New Testament uses for "convert" or "converted" is *epistrepho*, which means "to revert, come again, or turn about." Conversion is a 180-degree turn in one's concepts and conduct. This took some time in Saul, who was called Paul shortly after his acceptance by the church as a convert.

An initial step in Paul's "about-face" was accepting Jesus' statement "I am Jesus, whom you are persecuting" (Acts 9:5). There must have broken upon his consciousness, however dimly and indistinctly, the great truth that he more perfectly apprehended in later days: the truth that Christ and the church were one. It was as though Christ had said to him, "Those men and women whom you have dragged to prison have suffered; but it is I who have suffered in their suffering, Saul. The brutal stones that you saw hurled at Stephen, cutting into his flesh, reached Me and hurt Me. I felt every throb of Stephen's pain. Saul, you need to know that I am in My church individually and corporately. What you do on earth is felt in heaven." This was pure revelation to Saul of Tarsus.

Step two in this turnaround was the command "Arise and go into the city, and you will be told what you must do" (Acts 9:6). Paul, who was used to giving orders, was having to learn to take orders, even if they were unpleasant. Going into Damascus would not be an easy thing to do under the circumstances, for Paul had come as an emissary of the high priest to persecute the church, and now he was entering the city as a captive slave of the Lord Jesus Christ. Neither the Christians nor the Jews would want to receive him.

The third step was blindness produced by the radiant glory of Christ's appearance. Ezekiel called it "the glory of the Lord," and the rabbis called it the *shekinah* of God. Paul insisted that he saw more than brightness, for when he was listing the appearances of Christ after His resurrection he concluded, "Then last of all He was seen by me also, as by one born out of due time" (1 Cor. 15:8). Paul put this manifestation of Jesus on a par with those to Peter and James and the other apostles. This sight of Jesus was confirmed by Ananias's reference to "the Lord Jesus, who appeared to you on the road as you came..." (Acts 9:17). The last thing Paul saw before going blind was Jesus, and for the next three days he saw nothing but the memory of that appearance.

Being blind, a defeated, captured Paul was led into Damascus. Campbell Morgan has commented on this, "I think when I get to heaven I shall want to know what became of the high priest's letters" (*Acts of the Apostles*).

Paul had long known the *name* of Jesus, but he was terribly mistaken about the *nature* of the Lord. He had developed his own ideas and impressions of Christ, but not the right ones. He was totally destitute of the truth about Jesus, and to Agrippa he testified, "Indeed, I myself thought I must do many things contrary to the name of Jesus of Nazareth. This I also did in Jerusalem, and many of the saints I shut up in prison, having received authority from the chief priests; and when they were put to death, I cast my vote against them" (Acts 26:9,10). He was blind to Christ before he met Jesus, and then he was blinded by Christ for a season. Because Paul needed time to turn his mind around, Christ blazed an imprint of Himself upon Paul's consciousness.

A fourth step in this conversion process was the three days of solitude in the house on Straight Street. Paul had been so humiliated by being thrown to the ground in front of his soldiers and so shocked by the light and divine voice that he needed time to work himself through it. He was shut in with God, allowing God time to work radical changes in his mind and spirit.

There are times when we meet God in the dynamic revelations of His glory, and there are other times when we meet God best in the quiet solitude of meditation and reflection. Too often the supernatural visitations of

God are followed by frenzied activity rather than by thoughtful reflection. It is good to dwell awhile with the Spirit when He begins a work in us. It might be profitable if all new converts could be sequestered in a darkened room without food and water for three days until their experience with God is worked through their consciousness to their spirit and they become comfortable with their newfound relationship. Vivid impressions need the staying effect of reflection. These spiritual impressions must be faced and looked at so that they can be recognized again.

A fifth step in Paul's conversion was the intervention of Ananias, whom God had instructed to find Paul in Judas's house on Straight Street and to pray for him. The marvel of this story is how natural the supernatural seemed to those early Christians. Ananias expressed no surprise that the voice of the Lord had been heard by Saul. Jesus was accepted as alive from the dead, and Ananias was not shocked when he heard Him speak, nor was he surprised at anything that He had to say. Ananias heard and obeyed God's voice naturally and immediately.

Had Paul expected anyone, it would not have been this humble believer, who is called merely "a disciple." Ananias had no official position; he was not even a deacon. A reading of the Acts of the Apostles will show how independent of apostles the Holy Spirit was. He sent the deacon Philip to Samaria; it was the prayer of the deacon Stephen that arrested Saul of Tarsus; and here it was just a "believer" who was sent by God to lay hands on the man who was about to become the apostle to the Gentiles. Paul's healing, baptism and commission came through the obedient action of this disciple.

How much latent power lies unused in the hands of believers who have never been told that Christ wants to use them even though they have no official title in religious circles. Paul may have anticipated pomp and circumstance, but what he got was power and a commission. From the very beginning God taught Paul to receive ministry from whatever vessel He chooses to use.

The sixth step in his conversion was the restoration of sight. Ananias entered Paul's room with the greeting "Brother Saul" (Acts 9:17). This must have been consoling to Paul, who was no doubt wondering where he would fit in God's scheme of things. Then this disciple laid hands upon Saul, and "immediately there fell from his eyes something like scales, and he received his sight at once" (Acts 9:18). Not only were the scales of blindness removed, but "he received his sight." The years of groping for spiritual illumination were now over. Paul was given spiritual vision; his "inner" eyes were opened to see truths that had not been seen and recorded by men who preceded him. So much of the New Testament came into being as the result of this spiritual sight that God imparted to Paul through Ananias.

Paul's seventh step was a dual baptism. Ananias affirmed that God's purpose was "that you may receive your sight and be filled with the Holy Spirit" (Acts 9:17). Surely God did not just open Paul's eyes, for God's purposes are not half-fulfilled. Paul was Spirit-indwelt from this moment forward; therefore he was Spirit-led and Spirit-taught until the day of his execution. Paul learned to "live in the Spirit," "walk in the Spirit" and be "led by the Spirit," as he later instructed the Galatians to do (see Gal. 5).

With Paul's conversion, the landmark of history changed. He stands before us as remarkable in many ways: as an apostle; as a writer of many epistles; as a first missionary to the Gentiles; and as a most bold preacher of the gospel. He was the planter and settler of so many primitive churches far and wide and was a man of such endurances and of so many hairbreadth escapes that we might say he lived a charmed life.

Paul's conversion turned him from a person headed north to a man marching south. He had a name change from Saul—the Hebrew form—to Paul—the Gentile form—and a nature change that transformed a persecutor into a preacher and a murderer into a missionary. All of this came about because Paul met God in Christ Jesus and discovered that this Jesus indwelt the lives of believers.

Subsequent to the metamorphosis of Paul, "he arose and was baptized" (Acts 9:18), following both the example and the command of our Lord to be baptized in water. Then he was briefly presented to the disciples at Damascus before going into the Arabian desert for two or three years to work further through this radical conversion of spirit, mind and calling. Solitude is one of God's favorite tools for effecting sweeping changes in a person. Perhaps our rejection of solitude in America is reflected in the shallowness of our spiritual concepts. It takes time alone with God to come to know Him.

Paul's Changed Concepts

As touching his eternal destiny, Paul was soundly converted when he submitted his will and life to the lordship of Jesus Christ, for he later wrote, "If you confess with your mouth the Lord Jesus and believe in your heart that God has raised Him from the dead, you will be saved" (Rom. 10:9), but his theologically trained mind had some unlearning to do and much relearning to accept. Paul's concept of God was basically Hebrew, but it must have been colored by the Greek culture in which he had been raised. Even in his Hebrew religious culture, three erroneous views of God were common: one, that God is a limited being dwelling in temples and desiring our gifts (this seemed to be reinforced by the temple and all its ritualistic sacrifices); two, that God is an infinite being but is very removed from us—the creator but not the moral governor of the world (the dominance of Rome strengthened this concept that humans, not God, governed the world); three, that He is, of course, the only being, but all else is merely an extension of Him so that there is no separate existence, no responsibility, no sin and no personal holiness (this would not fit Paul's Pharisaic training, but it was popular among the Hellenistic Sadducees).

Wrong concepts, even if rejected, need the correction of truth, or they will war against what is thought to be correct. Peter realized this, for he wrote, "But sanctify the Lord God in your hearts, and always be ready to give a defense to everyone who asks you a reason for the hope that is in you, with meekness and fear" (1 Peter 3:15). Faith in God is not unreasonable, and the nature of God has been displayed across the pages of the Bible so an honest seeker can find substance for his or her faith. During the long months of solitude Paul spent in the desert area around Sinai, he reflected upon what he knew of the Scriptures and developed a theism that was threefold: we are in Christ; Christ is in us corporately; and Christ is in us individually.

Paul explained his first concept of the nature of God

when speaking to the Athenians on Mars' hill. He said, "For in Him we live and move and have our being" (Acts 17:28), and in saying this he moved God out of a man-made temple into the world as its creator and preserver, and established that He is not far from any of us but rather is everywhere present, observing, directing and controlling all things. Paul saw God as One on whom we are dependent and to whom we are responsible.

Paul came to realize that apart from Christ our lives would decay and be inert and helpless. Perhaps no words in the Bible better express our constant dependence on God than "for in Him we live and move." Christ is the original fountain of life, and He upholds us each moment. We owe to Him the ability to perform even the slightest motion. Paul was sharing his inspired revelation that our very existence is Christ's gift, and our power to move is equally His gift.

Paul traced our dependence upon Christ from the lowest pulsation of life to the highest powers of action and of continued existence. Actually our lives are but borrowed, for Paul wrote, "Do you not know that your body is the temple of the Holy Spirit who is in you, whom you have from God, and you are not your own?" and "For us there is only one God, the Father, of whom are all things, and we for Him; and one Lord Jesus Christ, through whom are all things, and through whom we live" (1 Cor. 6:19; 8:6). We are in the Father, from whom all life comes; we are in the Son, whose life we share; and we are in the Spirit, who is the breath of all flesh.

Since God is everywhere, and in Him we move, speak, act, think and live, God is nearer, closer, dearer and fuller far more than many Christians dare to conceive. God willed before the foundation of the world to make us one with Himself in Christ. He planned that we should be in the very closest union of love which created beings are capable of experiencing. For this purpose Jesus, in eternal harmony with the Father's will, took the manhood into God. When men saw our Lord Jesus Christ in the body, they saw Him who was not man only, but God; they saw Him who was, with the Father, one God. This oneness with us both reconciled us to God by putting away the Father's wrath and united us to God in Himself. "He who is joined to the Lord is one spirit with Him," Paul wrote (1 Cor. 6:17), and John affirmed the same truth in declaring, "He who abides in love abides in God, and God in him" (1 John 4:16). The New Testament uses the expression "in Christ" 164 times. Perhaps we should begin to believe it and live accordingly. Everywhere we go, He goes!

Paul's second conceptual change regarding God is an extension of the first: he saw Christ in the lives of believers corporately. Once Paul could accept that redeemed mankind has a very personal involvement with Jehovah through Jesus, it was but a logical progression for him to see that Christ dwells in the believers collectively. Paul's training in the Old Testament had taught him that after Adam and Eve's expulsion from Eden, God related to families, to tribes and to the entire nation of Israel. It wouldn't have been so difficult for him to see that Jesus also has a relationship to the corporate body.

As Paul developed his concept of Christ-in-us collectively, he expressed it in at least three major ways: Christ in His family; Christ in His temple; and Christ in His church.

In seeing believers as the family of God, Paul wrote, "Now, therefore, you are...members of the household of God" (Eph. 2:19), and lest we think of ourselves as servants in that household, he repeatedly called us children of God, saying, "The Spirit Himself bears witness with our spirit that we are children of God, and if children, then heirs—heirs of God and joint heirs with Christ" (Rom. 8:16,17). The broad expanse of Paul's concept of the family of God is expressed in this prayer: "For this reason I bow my knees to the Father of our Lord Jesus Christ, from whom the whole family in heaven and earth is named" (Eph. 3:14,15). Part of God's great family is already in heaven, glorified, while the rest of the family is here on earth being glorified. What a family!

"Children," "sons," "heirs" and "family" all speak of an intimate relationship, but they also speak of something far more precious. As friends of God we are objects of His divine love, but as children of God we are partakers of His divine nature. We bear His image and likeness. We are indwelt by His Spirit of life, and we carry the family name wherever we go. Paul stated, "For whom He foreknew, He also predestined to be conformed to the image of His Son, that He might be the firstborn among many brethren" (Rom. 8:29), and "As we have borne the image of the man of dust, we shall also bear the image of the heavenly Man" (1 Cor. 15:49). We do not develop into children of God; we are born into the family of God and develop maturity in Christ as the children of God. Much of Paul's epistles concerns this development and maturation of the Christ-like nature that was imparted to us at the new birth. Christ's nature is seen in His family.

As Paul developed his converted concepts of God's nature dwelling in the believers collectively, he visualized us as the temple of God. "Do you not know that you are the temple of God and that the Spirit of God dwells in you?" he wrote (1 Cor. 3:16), and later added, "For you are the temple of the living God. As God has said: 'I will dwell in them and walk among them. I will be their God, and they shall be My people'" (2 Cor. 6:16). Contrary to our Western idea of a church building being a place for a congregation to assemble, the concept of a temple in Old Testament times was a place for God to dwell. Paul built on this image by writing, "...in whom [Jesus Christ] the whole building, being joined together, grows into a holy temple in the Lord, in whom you also are being built together for a habitation of God in the Spirit" (Eph. 2:21,22).

One person does not constitute a temple, but God has chosen to fit us together, as a master mason cuts stones to fit into a wall, and in our collective unit we become a special habitation in which God can reside through His Spirit. This has nothing to do with local church structures, for God does not dwell in buildings made by men; He inhabits the temple put together by Himself.

The temple had three primary functions: it was the residence of God; it was a place of access to God; and it was a place for worship of God to ascend. The collective believers of our generation exist for the same purposes. God, who walked with Adam in the garden in the cool of the day, now chooses to reside in His holy temple: the believers. The days of tents and stone structures are over. God resides in a living building. He prefers the lives of His saints to the finest architecture on the face of this earth. He is a living God who dwells in a living temple.

Since this is true, access to God will be through this temple. Men and women will meet God in Christ-indwelt men and women. The world's concept of God is formed by viewing the lives of the Christians in their circle of acquaintances. Speaking to the Corinthians as a whole, Paul said, "Do you not know that your body is the temple of the Holy Spirit who is in you, whom you have from God, and you are not your own? For you were bought at a price; therefore glorify God in your body and in your spirit, which are God's" (1 Cor. 6:19,20). Men meet God in His temple and we, collectively, are that place of meeting.

Just like Solomon's temple, today's believers are the place where praise, worship and adoration are offered up to God. Sacrifices of praise are brought to His temple. Gifts of thanksgiving are presented to God in His earthly temple, and the ointment of adoration is poured upon the head of Christ in this temple. If believers do not worship God when they come together to form the temple, where will they worship? God will never be worshipped in the chambers of commerce, nor will the halls of entertainment extol the blessed name of the Lord Jesus. It is in God's temple—the collective body of believers—that God is to be worshipped.

Paul's thinking took a slight turn when he shifted from calling the collective believers the "temple of God" and began to refer to them as the "church of God." Paul must have loved this concept, for he referred to the church more than eighty times in his epistles. He spoke of the temple as being the place of God's residence on earth, but he projected the church as the body of Christ on the earth (see Col. 1:18,24) and visualized individual believers as being members, or functioning units, of that body. He graphically described this in 1 Corinthians 12, and he summarized by saying, "Now you are the body of Christ, and members individually" (verse 27).

At the manger in Bethlehem, God provided Christ a body that could die, and it died gloriously. From the tomb outside Jerusalem, God brought forth a glorified body that could live, and Christ lives as the God-man throughout all eternity in the heavens. But on the day of Pentecost, God provided Christ a body that could function on this earth: the church. As surely as Christ inhabited the body on the cross and the body that rose from the tomb, He inhabits His body on the earth. He is now doing everything He did while He was on this earth, but now He is doing it through the believers. Luke began the Acts of the Apostles with the statement "The former account I made, O Theophilus, of all that Jesus began both to do and teach" (Acts 1:1), implying that what he was now writing was all that Jesus continued to do and to teach. The early disciples had no concept of Christ being separated from His body. They honored Him as the head of that body, and they obeyed Him implicitly and immediately.

Christ has not changed; it is only our concepts that have changed. As long as we visualize Christ as being confined to the throne in heaven, we will continue to do His work *for* Him on the earth. If we could catch Paul's representation of Christ residing in His church on earth and functioning as its head, we would return to working *with* God. It goes without saying that the church has always been more successful working *with* God than working *for* God. With Christ as the head of the church, His Spirit as the actuating principle and the believers as the functioning members of that body, there should be no limit to what can be accomplished in the here and now.

As revelation after revelation flooded over Paul's consciousness, he progressed from seeing us in Christ to seeing Christ in us collectively, but eventually he began to accept that Christ is in us as individuals whether we are Jew or Gentile. Sometime during his season of divine disclosures, the wonderful announcement that the offer of salvation was not confined, as he had once supposed, to the Jewish people, but that all men were invited into God's grace, dawned upon Paul's mind like a brilliant sunrise after a long, dark night. It became the great truth that so animated the heart and fired the zeal of this apostle. Excitedly he wrote of "Christ in you, the hope of glory" (Col. 1:27).

The context of this verse deals with the mystery of the gospel—the previously unrevealed truth that God's glory would be made manifest in and through the Gentiles. Daniel saw this in shadow, but Paul saw it in substance. To Paul's mind, this mystery was wrapped up in Jesus. He is one of the persons of the mystery of the Trinity, and He is the mystery of the gospel, for the mystery of His divine Sonship, His divine person—being both God and man in one person—and His incarnation and redemption form the major part of the gospel. Paul could hardly contain his excitement—realizing that this Christ, who is the sum and substance of the gospel, is *in* His people not only as an omnipresent God, the creator in whom we "live and move and have our being," but in a way of special grace.

This phrase "Christ in you" is expressive of a revelation of Christ in believers, of their possession of His presence and person, and of His living in them by His Spirit. It speaks of the communion available to believers because of their union with Christ.

Most translators agree that the Greek preposition used here—*en*—needs to be translated as "in," signifying the indwelling of Christ in the hearts of individual believers by His Spirit. Some commentators, however, prefer to translate *en* as "among," emphasizing the great wonder that Christ is proclaimed among the Gentiles. The difference is actually minor, for the real emphasis is upon the *you*. To Paul, the surest demonstration that Christ was among the Gentiles was the evident fact that He was *in* the hearts of the Colossians. Paul could conceive of no other way by which Christ could be present among the Gentiles collectively except by indwelling individual believers.

It was not only the Colossians who were so divinely indwelt, for Paul wrote to the Galatian Christians, "My little children, for whom I labor in birth again until Christ is formed in you" (Gal. 4:19), and he reminded the Thessalonians, "He comes, in that Day, to be glorified in His saints" (2 Thess. 1:10).

Christianity is Christ in the heart. Paul prayed "that Christ may dwell in your hearts through faith" (Eph. 3:17), and he testified, "Christ lives in me" (Gal. 2:20). He asked the Corinthian believers, "Do you not know yourselves, that Jesus Christ is in you?" (2 Cor. 13:5). He could say this because Jesus, in His high priestly prayer, had declared to the Father, "I in them, and You in Me; that they may be perfect in one" (John 17:23), and had added, "that the love with which You loved Me may be in them, and I in them" (John 17:26).

Anything less than this is not New Testament

Christianity. Christian theory, doctrine, practice and fellowship all have their place, but the central core of the Christian experience forever remains "Christ in you!" Unless Christ inhabits the lives of believers, their faith is vain and they are still in their sins, no matter how religious they may seem or how righteously they may live. It is not our behavior that makes us Christians; it is the indwelling Christ who makes us saints and changes our outer behavior.

As Jesus revealed Himself to Paul—first outside Damascus, then in Judas's house on Straight Street inside Damascus, and again during Paul's sojourn in the Sinai peninsula—He seemed to impress a specific point upon this righteously perfect keeper of the Law: people must depend on divine grace, truth and love rather than upon Jewish (or, later, Christian) ceremonies, personal suffering or philosophic speculation to strengthen their confidence in a hope of glory, whether earthly or heavenly. "Christ in you [is] the hope of glory" was the revelation. All future glory, including heaven, and whatever sharing in Christ's glory we may experience here on the earth, is wrapped up in Christ Jesus. "We have this treasure in earthen vessels," Paul declared (2 Cor. 4:7).

"Glory" is among the greatest words in our language, and it is one of God's most magnificent titles. Christ is revealed as the hope of glory, and this hope is both a promise and a provision of seeing the glory of the Lord fulfilled in and revealed through us. Even David pondered this as he sang, "What is man that You are mindful of him, and the son of man that You visit him?... You have crowned him with glory and honor" (Ps. 8:4,5).

Glorious things belong to the realm of glory, and where Christ is and where He reigns as Lord is the place of divine splendor. In the Old Testament, God declared, "I am the Lord, that is My name; and My glory I will not give to another" (Is. 42:8), but in the provisions of the New Covenant, Christ prayed to the Father, "The glory which You gave Me I have given them, that they may be one just as We are one" (John 17:22), and Paul affirmed, "God...calls you into His own kingdom and glory" (1 Thess. 2:12). Christ has purchased glory for us, has actually taken possession of the glory for us and has pledged Himself to bring believers into His glory. Christ in us crowns us with His own divine glory, and this fact accords a firm hope that we will share in the fullness of the glory that is yet to be displayed. The Christ who has come to live with us will never leave us until we are glorified. Hallelujah!

So the circle has been completed. Adam was clothed with the glory of the Lord, but he lost it through sin. Subsequently, Noah met a measure of that glory in a speaking God; Abraham, in a covenant made by God; and Moses, in the display of the moral nature of God. Joshua found divine glory in the power of God, and Isaiah met it in the holiness of God. Ezekiel saw this glory as the departing *shekinah*, and Daniel sensed it in the many revelations of God. Peter met the glory of the Lord in the God-man, in whom "we beheld His glory, the glory as of the only begotten of the Father" (John 1:14), and John the beloved entered into a display of God's glory through receiving God's love.

Now the glory that once clothed Adam indwells believers. The fellowship Adam experienced with God has progressed to believers dwelling in God. Adam awaited God's presence in the cool of the day, but believers have the presence of God within them every moment of a twenty-four-hour day.

What was lost has been restored with vast improvements and enlargements. If Adam were allowed to look down from heaven, he could not keep from being jealous of the relationship God has restored to us in this hour. We have all that he had, plus Christ.

We have met God—and He is ours, and we are His!

OTHER PUBLICATIONS OF INTEREST FROM CREATION HOUSE

The Emerging Christian Woman
by Anne Gimenez

Women are on the move. They are shaking off many years of silence and passivity. Inspired by the Spirit, they are assuming their proper roles of leadership in the body of Christ. Anne believes Christ is calling Christian women to take a lead in bringing new life, healing and unity to the church. $4.95

Spiritual Power and Church Growth
by C. Peter Wagner

Why do some churches grow like wildfire? How can we learn from this marvelously successful church growth movement? C. Peter Wagner identifies the main reasons for the expansion of Pentecostal churches and articulates key principles behind their growth in Latin America. With examples, stories and facts, he writes about how to engage the power of the Holy Spirit; involving new Christians in ministry; cell groups; training leaders in service; the importance of signs and wonders; and other valuable principles. $6.95

Ministries Today is a practical bi-monthly journal for church leaders. Whether you're a pastor, music leader, deacon, youth minister or active lay leader you'll find every issue offers you practical helps and advice on administrative, pastoral and educational issues. *Ministries Today*'s articles carefully blend proven leadership techniques with spiritual sensitivity.

Ministries Today will help you meet the challenges of contemporary church leadership in a stress-filled world. You will gain insights from resources and specialists in the areas of counseling, communications and administration—financial advisors, builders, tax experts, medical and legal professionals and others with specific expertise in church-related matters.

Ministries Today is right on target, addressing tough topics and providing practical and proven leadership insights with each issue.

Become a well-informed leader and subscribe now to *Ministries Today*. Send just $18 to: *Ministries Today*, P.O. Box 881, Farmingdale, NY 11737. You'll receive a full year (six issues) of practical, sensible insight and advice. Order today.